The Essential Beginner's Guide To
MEDITATION &
MINDFULNESS

Achieve Clarity, Wisdom, Happiness,
and Peace; Relieve Stress, Anxiety,
and Panic Attacks to Improve
Your Mental Health

Rohini Heendeniya

Phoenix
epublishing

Published by Phoenix ePublishing
www.phoenixepublishing.com
Cover design by Angela Alaya
First Edition: June 2023

TABLE OF CONTENTS

INTRODUCTION

"To know oneself is the beginning of wisdom" –
Socrates

Imagine yourself at the edge of a large ocean. You take a deep breath and feel the salty air fill your lungs as the waves crash gently and rhythmically against the coast. You move forward while closing your eyes and stepping into the sand. You start to feel at ease as the world around you disappears. This is how it feels to meditate.

The practice of meditation involves clearing your thoughts and concentrating on the present moment. It has been demonstrated that this ancient technique has many positive effects on both physical and mental health. But what does meditation entail?

When you meditate, you are training your mind to be more focused and attentive. Instead of allowing your thoughts and emotions to rule your life, you take charge of them. Just like lifting weights, the more you do it, the stronger your mind becomes.

There are many ways to meditate, such as sitting quietly or mindfully moving your body. While some find it beneficial to focus on breathing, others prefer using mantras or visualization exercises. Finding what works for you and incorporating meditation into your daily routine are key; there is no right or wrong way.

Regardless of age or background, anyone can learn and practice meditation and mindfulness because they are basic life skills. It doesn't call for particular ideologies or certain gear or tools. All you need for your practice is yourself, your intention, and your presence at that moment. You may add some things, such as a cushion or seating pad to help you stay seated comfortably, light a fragrant candle, or even burn incense.

I recognize that starting a meditation and mindfulness practice can be difficult, so this book for beginners is designed to assist you in overcoming any barriers that may be in your way. If you are dealing with stress, anxiety, or other mental health difficulties, this book will give you a road map to help you start your journey to better mental health.

I will walk you through easy steps, techniques, and strategies for meditation, helping you build a habit and gain a profound understanding of yourself over time by practicing daily. The ease of the practice will improve your health and vitality. Practicing meditation and mindfulness is understanding and living with compassion and knowledge, both for yourself and everyone in your life.

In addition to bringing about peace and harmony, the practice also profoundly changes unhealthful conditions of the body and mind. Numerous studies have shown conclusively how regular meditation affects, heals, and improves the mind and body. You'll become more active and engaged in your life as a result.

For many people, problems with stress, anxiety, panic attacks, and depression are getting worse. This can result from chronic stress. Although our modern culture and pace of life provide benefits, they also put us under increased pressure. We are often unsure how to handle life's stressors effectively without becoming overwhelmed.

Stress at some levels might be beneficial. It can inspire people and propel planned actions toward successful completion. However, life isn't always so simple or lucid. For many people, stress has become a constant in their experience. When juggling multiple aspects of a busy life (a career, finances, children, marriage, parents, home, etc.), stress levels can rise and become chronic, making it difficult to cope or deal with life's responsibilities healthily and beneficially.

While some may feel that meditation is incompatible with their way of life, you can learn to meditate and engage in other mindfulness exercises without necessarily incorporating a certain belief system into your practice. But perhaps it's important to remember that Buddhist values like kindness, gratitude, and compassion are mirrored in other major belief systems and are universal.

I have a lifelong relationship with the philosophies of Buddhism and therefore with meditation as it is an intrinsic part of its practice. As an experienced alternative therapies practitioner and life coach, utilizing Emotional Freedom Technique™ (EFT), Kinesiology, Past Life Regression Therapy, Tibetan Acupressure Massage, Swedish Body Massage, and other complementary spiritual therapies, I understand the therapeutic benefits of regular meditation and mindfulness.

With a deep understanding of the challenges beginners face, I have taken great care in crafting this book to be approachable, useful, and easy to follow. I draw on the most recent scientific research and share my own experiences and insights to explain the benefits of mindfulness and meditation practices and offer evidence-based tools and strategies to help you reach your goals.

This is a perfect book for anybody with the desire to begin meditation and mindfulness practice or deepen their understanding of these techniques, regardless of experience level. This book will help you attain clarity, wisdom, happiness, and peace, and relieve stress and anxiety to enhance your mental health. It uses practical tools and techniques, clear language, and an evidence-based approach. This book will give you the direction and support you need to accomplish your goals.

Before we go any further, please note, the knowledge in this book is not meant to replace professional or medical advice, diagnosis, or treatment. The descriptions of physical and mental health issues included in this book are generalizations, not diagnoses for any specific individual. I urge you to get expert medical advice from a qualified healthcare provider if you exhibit signs of a physical or mental health condition.

While it has been demonstrated that mindfulness and meditation techniques can help people reduce stress and anxiety and improve their general mental health, the specific effects of these practices may vary from person to person. It is crucial to remember that mindfulness and meditation techniques should not be used in place of expert medical care for any physical or mental health condition. I sincerely hope this book proves useful to you in your quest for improved mental health and well-being.

Chapter One

A HISTORY OF MEDITATION AND MINDFULNESS

*"When a man knows the solitude of
silence and feels the joy of quietness, he
is then free from fear and he feels joy."*
– Buddha

Sit still, focus on your breathing, and reflect—that's the idea of meditation. However, meditation has a rich cultural history that has seen it evolve from a religious concept to something that may now appear more stylish than spiritual.

According to a quote attributed to French philosopher Michel de Montaigne, "A person's ability to belong to themselves is the best thing in the world."

This couldn't be more accurate in our modern, fast-paced environment. It requires conscious effort to take a moment and give ourselves the time we need to examine who we truly are when there are so many demands on our minds and time. Even when we do find the time, many people struggle to actually do this. There is no doubt that meditation practice is a significant strategy that can be beneficial.

The word meditation comes from the Latin *meditatum*, which means "to ponder." Through the practice of meditation, we can aim to find a closer connection with our body in the ordinary moments that we often let pass us by and develop a stronger awareness of how our emotions influence our actions.

You might already have a successful meditation routine, or you might be new to the practice and seeking to expand your knowledge and understanding of the benefits meditation can have on your day-to-day activities. In either case, it's fascinating to learn about the history of meditation.

Where Did Meditation Originate?

Finding the actual origin of meditation is equally difficult as determining how long it has been practiced.

The earliest written documents date back to Hindu traditions of Vendatism in India, which date to roughly 1500 BCE. Vendatism, a philosophical system, is one of the earliest known Indian pathways to spiritual enlightenment. Then, other forms of meditation from Taoist China and Buddhist India in the sixth and fifth centuries BCE are cited.

There is much discussion over the exact origins, particularly in relation to Buddhist meditation. The sutras of the Pāli Canon, which date back to the first century BCE, provide some of the first written accounts of the various states of meditation practiced in India at the time of early Buddhism. The Pāli Canon is a selection of Theravada Buddhist scriptures.

There is also some evidence linking Judaism to meditation activities, which are said to have been passed down from the religion's earliest traditions. A description of the patriarch Isaac heading to "lasuach" in a field can be found in the Hebrew Bible or Torah, which consists of the first five books of the Tanakh. Most people understand this phrase to refer to a certain type of meditation.

Who Created/Invented Meditation?

Some of the information we have points to a core group of individuals who have played a significant role in popularizing meditation. However, there are many more who were as significant in spreading and sharing the practice of meditation; I've listed three of them below:

India's Buddha

The Buddha, also called Siddhartha Gautama or Siddhattha Gotama in Pāli, was a prince who later attained the status of monk, sage, philosopher, and religious figure. Buddhism was established in accordance with his teachings.

As a result, it may be easy to assume that the Buddha conceived or produced meditation, but this is not the case. Buddhist writings make reference to a wide variety of meditation techniques, and the Buddha sought out other enlightened teachers to acquire the practice and paths to self-fulfillment. Although he played a major role in popularizing meditation as a practice, the Buddha did not create it.

China's Lao-Tze

Lao-Tze, also known by the names Lao-Tzu and Laozi, was an old Chinese philosopher whose name is primarily an honorific title that means "Old Teacher" or "Old Master."

He is credited with writing the Tao-te-Ching, a textual representation of his ideas and teachings that served as the foundation for the Taoist philosophy, which emphasizes meditation techniques and the concept of knowledge in silence. There is great debate over whether Lao-Tze was a single person or if the name refers to a group of people and philosophers who held similar beliefs.

Japan's Dosho

Dosho, a Japanese monk, traveled to China in the 7th century to study Buddhism under Hsuan Tsang, a revered teacher of the time. Dosho acquired all of his knowledge of the Zen way of life during this tour, bringing it with him when he returned to Japan.

He opened his first Zazen meditation hall when he got back, which is a type of sitting meditation. In Japan, he established a community of monks and pupils with the main goal of passing along this type of meditation.

Meditation's Origin and History

Despite the fact that meditation is fairly prevalent and often practiced today, it's important to recognize that its roots and history are deep. Exploring the origins of meditation will help you gain a deeper understanding of the practice's rich diversity and how it developed across different nations and eras. Meditation has been and is still being modified to fit our lives today.

I've outlined these origins and roots briefly below:

Yogis, India, and Vendatism

The earliest known illustrations of meditation come from India and date from about 5000 and 3500 BCE. Wall art paintings show people seated in meditative-like positions with their eyes half closed, seemingly deep in meditation.

The first known text on meditation can be traced back to India, specifically the Hindu Vendatism traditions, and dates to roughly 1500 BCE. It's vital to remember that even though the Vedas wrote literature outlining meditation techniques, these had long since been transmitted orally through storytelling customs.

Hindu texts also mention the Yogi practice of meditation in caves in addition to the Vedic practice. Many contemporary meditation approaches, including the current yoga movement, whose methods are largely based on the Hatha Yoga practice, are thought to have their origins in this tradition.

It's important to realize that these techniques' roots are not in the usual stretching and movement that many Western schools now teach but rather in meditation for spiritual development.

Indian Buddhism

Meditation is often most strongly associated with Buddhism, even though the picture of the Buddha sitting in meditation on a lotus flower didn't emerge until much later after Buddhism itself had already started. Buddhism's classical vocabulary refers to meditation as bhvan, which means mental progress, or dhyna, which means mental tranquility.

There are numerous meditation methods and exercises. Three other practices, each with its unique approach to meditation, also emerged about the same time that Buddhism was expanding. Despite not being as well-known as Buddhism on a worldwide scale, these are nonetheless important to be aware of:

- **Mahavira and Jainism in India**

  The Tirthankara Mahavira, also known as Vardhamna, is credited with bringing back Jainism in India. The word "Tirthankara," which means "Ford Maker," designates the creator of a "tirtha," a passageway through the sea of births and deaths. The twenty-fourth Tirthankara was Mahavira. He promoted the moral and spiritual teachings of the Tirthankaras from the pre-Vedic period, which sparked India's return to Jainism. As a way of life, Jainism strongly emphasizes non-violence, self-control, and contemplation. Jainism's meditation practices put a special emphasis on mantras, visualizations, and breathing.

- **Lao Tze and Taoism in China**

  Although it is debatable whether Lao Tze was a single person or whether the term refers to a group of people, it is assumed that he existed sometime in the 6th century BCE. Taoism emphasizes integrating with "Tao," which refers to "cosmic life" or nature. Focusing on mindfulness, pausing for thought, and using imagery are all part of the traditional Taoist meditation practices.

- **Confucianism and Confucius in China**

  Confucius was a Chinese philosopher, teacher, and politician who lived in the sixth century BCE. His ideas and teachings were embodied in the Confucianism school of philosophy, which is still widely practiced in China today. Confucianism emphasizes morality, social justice, and one's development. Confucianism refers to meditation as Jing Zuo, which focuses on introspection and self-improvement.

Sufism and the practice of meditation

Sufism is a long-standing Islamic practice that has been around for at least 1400 years. Muslims engage in this practice in order to establish a spiritual connection with Allah (God) through introspection, meditation, and renunciation of worldly possessions. Sufism is said to have developed its unique form of meditation, which focuses on breathing and employs mantras through some Indian influence.

Judaism and the practice of meditation

The Jewish esoteric philosophy and school of thought known as Kabbalah also include some of its own types of meditation in addition to what is claimed to be descriptions of meditation practice in the Torah. These typically center on in-depth reflection on philosophical issues and prayer.

Meditation's Spread in the West

The practice of meditation has primarily been linked in modern times to Asian spiritual traditions like Tibetan Buddhism, Zen, and Theravada. Due to colonialism and improved means of communication and transportation, Western interest in Eastern religions and philosophies appears to have started in earnest in the 19th century. It was primarily the purview of academics and missionaries back then.

Western "seekers" and artists first grew interested in Eastern philosophy in the late 19th century, but it wasn't until the mid-20th century that meditation gained popularity in the West. During this time, Eastern meditation gurus arrived and were welcomed to teach interested students about their techniques and knowledge.

Many Western students of mindfulness had the opportunity to go east and study with great masters in countries like India, Thailand, Burma, and other parts of Asia; then return home and spread what they had learned about mindfulness and awareness techniques.

Dr. Jon Kabat-Zinn, who established the University of Massachusetts Medical School's Center for

Mindfulness in 1979, is one of the field's most significant figures today. His MBSR (Mindfulness-Based Stress Reduction) program has been crucial in bringing the advantages of mindfulness practice to the public's awareness and the scientific community around the world.

Since its inception about 30 years ago, MBSR has gained popularity. These days, "mindfulness" seems to be in every place. Although there are many different forms of mindfulness, such as "mindful snacks," "mindful juice bars," and "mindful pants," nothing compares to the classic mindfulness of being totally present with what is.

Meditation and Religion

Meditation techniques are used in every religion. While numerous faiths share the same core beliefs, each has its own direction, drawing on its own unique symbols, tales, and teachings and emphasizing particular rituals, topics, and goals.

Meditation is a practice that can be found in all five major world religions: Hinduism, Buddhism, Judaism, Christianity, and Islam.

Hinduism and meditation

The role of meditation can vary in different aspects of Indian spirituality, depending on the individual practitioner, his or her chosen path, and stage of life.

Hindu refers to India, a culturally rich and historically significant nation with numerous intertwined traditions, including Buddhism.

There is no single founder or text for Hinduism. Some of its key books include The Upanishads (a treatise on the essence of God), The Bhagavad Gita (a treatise on man's responsibility in the world), and The Ramayana and The Mahabharata (sagas that illustrate spiritual concepts through action).

India is well renowned for its distinctive contributions to the practice of yoga and the teachings that go along with it, the Patanjali Sutras.

Reincarnation is a core tenet of Hinduism's worldview. It would take several lives to fully experience all of the Hindu spiritual practices, including those of traveling ascetics, psychic performers, cloistered monks, and worshippers of particular deities.

Buddhism and meditation

Buddhism, a long-standing and diverse religion that offers the most well-developed forms of meditation, places such a strong emphasis on meditation that many people mistake it for purely Buddhist practice.

Buddhist techniques for meditation include silent sitting meditation (known as "zazen" in Zen Buddhism), focused attention on the breath (such as in Anapanasati meditation), loving-kindness meditation (Metta), mindfulness body sensations (body scan meditation), walking meditation (Khinhin), and contemplation of impermanence (Vipassana).

Siddhartha Gautama, a prince who abandoned his position in favor of ascetic life, is credited with founding Buddhism. His meditations led to his enlightenment as the Buddha. Right perspective, right determination, right speech, right behavior, right livelihood, right effort, right consciousness, and right meditation are the eight principles (The Noble Eightfold Path) that Buddha defined as developing a person's fully realized condition.

Buddhism has three main schools, as well as numerous minor ones. The Hinayana School (known as the "lesser vehicle"), which is primarily found in Asia and whose writings are written in Pali, seeks to enlighten its followers personally. Aiming to impart enlightenment to all sentient beings, the Mahayana School (known as the "greater vehicle") is mostly practiced in Tibet and Japan. Its texts are primarily written in Sanskrit. The most esoteric techniques are taught by the Vajrayana School, which is referred to as the "indestructible vehicle."

With the teachings of Bodhidharma, another prominent school, Zen Buddhism (a division of The Mahayana School), was founded in the sixth century. By shattering the illusions that are supported by traditional conceptions and philosophies and that shape our perceptions, expectations, and actions, Zen seeks to unveil the truth. The koan, a conundrum with no obvious solution, is a special type of meditation offered by Zen.

Judaism and meditation

The word "qabalah" in Hebrew has two meanings: to receive and to reveal. The Qabalah tradition is a symbolic language intended to advance practitioners' spiritual growth. It is both a metaphysical concept and philosophy. By internalizing symbols and gradually taking on their qualities through meditation, students of the Qabalah transform their essential inner natures with the essential exterior nature.

The primary emblem of the Qabalah is The Tree Of Life (Otz Chim), a cosmogram made up of eleven spheres (sephiroth), one of which is concealed and connected by twenty-two pathways. The Crown, Wisdom, Understanding, Knowledge, Severity, Mercy, Beauty, Victory, Glory, Foundation, and Kingdom are just a few of the different God names that each sephira carries. Each sephira is given a unique set of symbols, such as a title, name, image, color, and number.

Meditation arouses a person's higher powers, going beyond logic and bringing the symbols to life.

Christianity and meditation

Although some methods are not widely approved by all churches (including but not limited to Orthodox, Catholic, Lutheran, Baptist, Protestant, Episcopalian, Quaker, Shaker, and Gnostic), Christian meditation has a long history.

In order to assimilate the spiritual truths inherent in them, the Desert Fathers, early hermits who started the foundation for the Christian isolated life either individually or in groups, employed repeated prayer, either spoken or sung, with synchronized breathing. Icons are made and used as meditation objects in the Eastern Orthodox faiths.

The Jesuit traditions use vision and imagination to respond to situations from Christ's life, such as the Nativity, Passion, and Resurrection, in a deeply felt, personal way and internalize the lessons they contain. The repetition of prayers—individually, collectively, or in a cycle—is the most basic and widely applicable form of Christian meditation.

No matter how it is expressed—through singing, prayer, research, or contemplation—the heart is usually the first place the focus is directed, leading to a profound knowledge that permeates the entire self.

Islam and meditation

Islam's mystical path Sufism, which has its roots in the Koran and Muhammad's teachings, incorporates master commentaries and teachings from a variety of esoteric traditions, such as Zoroastrianism, Hermeticism, and Pythagoreanism.

It is further strengthened by a strong literary heritage that places emphasis on poetry, allegory, and symbolic narrative. Writing, calligraphy, geometry, architecture, dancing, weaving, and other commonplace activities transform to become vehicles for meditation as the arts reveal universal principles. Everything is revered, and there is unification everywhere.

Sufi spiritual practice places a strong emphasis on the pupil-teacher connection; only those who have been acknowledged as masters by earlier masters (in a lineage that dates back to the prophet) are permitted to initiate pupils.

Meditation practices prescribed by masters can take many different forms in their final iteration. Meditation (fikr) is meant to keep the mind from wandering while the heart is fixed on God. The repeated recitation of the Holy Names (zikr) in spoken word (prayer, chant, song) is strongly stressed as an active invocation of God.

Meditation and other religions

Many other spiritual traditions' practices are similar in form and purpose to these practices. And they provide a lot more. It is helpful to talk about how similar some of these techniques are.

Trance states, which often involve a loss of self-awareness, share common threads even though they may vary considerably. Similar to this, altered states of consciousness brought on by pharmacological agents can resemble one another in some respects while still being very different in others.

Rarely, if ever, does meditation result in a loss of self-awareness or self-control; on the contrary, it almost invariably heightens both.

Though meditation can take many different forms, all systems of meditation have certain basic principles. Through a variety of focus points, the entire being (body, mind, and emotion) is actively used to cultivate awareness, insight, and transformation.

Spiritual Benefits of Meditation

The spiritual benefits of meditation are accessible to even those of us who do not consider ourselves to be spiritual. The following may appear to have been divinely sourced to someone of a certain religious belief.

- Greater empathy
- Increased compassion
- A feeling of connection
- Mental stability and less emotional reactivity

- A feeling of tranquility, serenity, and inner peace
- Self-assurance, self-worth, and a desire to be sincere
- A strong sense of the meaning and significance of life
- Access to a constant inner source of happiness

Faith in any omnipotent power aside, faith in meditation practice is all that's needed to embody these qualities.

Chapter Two

THE FOUR FOUNDATIONS OF MINDFULNESS

"Those who make channels for water control the water; makers of arrows make the arrows straight; carpenters control their timber; and the wise control their own minds." - Buddha

This book incorporates the initial three foundations of mindfulness from Buddhist teachings, which beautifully outline the path and objective of meditation. It offers a precise method of contemplating the layers of awareness.

While the fourth application(dhammas) holds less relevance for this guide's intentions, it can be set aside for now.

In Buddhism, the one-way path to overcoming suffering and achieving nirvana is made up of the "four foundations of mindfulness". This phrase refers to the mindful examination of four objective domains: the body, feelings, states of mind, and dhammas. Together, these domains make up the entire field of human experience.

Meditation involves more than just mindfulness but the fusion of mindfulness, energy, and discernment, as well as detachment from the claims of the ordinary world.

In terms of the four foundations, the body's contemplation is concerned with the material side of life, the middle two are concerned with the mental side, and the final application is concerned with the investigation of experience in ways that represent the teaching's purpose. The four come into play in a specific order, with the body coming first.

First Foundation: Mindfulness of the Body

The first is breathing mindfulness. The Buddha himself utilized this meditation technique the night before he attained enlightenment, and he acclaimed it throughout his teaching career as "a pure happy abiding that drives away unhealthy thoughts as soon as they appear."

To engage in this practice, we gently observe the natural rhythm of our breath through the lens of mindfulness. As we breathe in and out through the nostrils, our focus rests upon the sensations near the upper lip or nostrils, where we can perceive the gentle flow of air entering and leaving the body. The mindfulness of breath brings us back from our mental rambles and firmly establishes the mind in the present. The Buddha succinctly stated: "Just mindful one breathes in, mindful one breathes out."

The sutta describes four stages in which mindfulness of breathing develops. Initially, we bring our attention to the length of our inhalations and exhalations, observing whether they naturally tend to be long or short in the first two stages.

As we advance into the third stage, our awareness expands to the full body in addition to in-and-out breathing. The fourth step is when we "calm the bodily function", allowing the breathing and other bodily functions to progressively become much more subtle.

Walking, standing, sitting, lying down, and changing from one posture to another are all included in the practice of mindfulness of the postures, which comes after contemplation of the body. As we engage in the practice of walking, standing, sitting or lying down, we cultivate a deep awareness of our actions in the present moment.

We acknowledge and embrace each posture we assume, recognizing that we are walking when we walk, standing when we stand, sitting when we sit, and lying down when we lie down. The body is shown to be an impersonal structure of living substance that is subject to the guiding impact of will when the postures are thought about.

The next exercise, referred to as mindfulness and clear comprehension, incorporates mindfulness into a variety of daily activities. We are fully aware of what we are doing and why we are doing it before performing any action. Thus, routine bodily functions like leaving and returning, looking ahead and away, bending and stretching the limbs, getting dressed, eating, drinking, carrying out bodily functions, sleeping, waking up, speaking, and being silent all become a part of the practice of cultivating mindfulness. The practice is totally integrated into daily living, and everyday life itself becomes a full-bodied practice.

Second Foundation: Mindfulness of Feeling

The contemplation of feeling is the next foundation of mindfulness. The word "feeling" in this context does not mean an emotion but rather the basic affective undertone of an experience, whether it is pleasant, unpleasant, or neutral.

Making a feeling the focus of mindfulness prevents it from evoking an unhealthy reaction and allows it to be perceived as just another impersonal aspect of existence.

We merely observe the various characteristics of the feelings as pleasant, painful, or neutral in the early phases of contemplating feelings. They are perceived as raw mental events devoid of all personal connotations and indications of an "I" who feels them. With further experience, one may tell if the emotion is worldly, leaning toward attachment, or spiritual, tending toward detachment.

Over time, the emphasis of attention moves from the intensity of the feelings to the actual process of feeling, which is revealed to be a never-ending flux of feelings that arise and vanish one after another without pausing.

As it develops, an understanding of impermanence overturns the craving for pleasurable feelings, aversion to painful emotions, and misconception over neutral emotions.

Third Foundation: Mindfulness of Mind

Contemplation of the mind, or the observation of mental states, is the third foundation of mindfulness.

The Buddha listed sixteen mental states under this contemplation, which are divided into eight pairs:

- the mind with lust and the mind without lust;

- the mind with aversion and the mind without aversion;
- the mind with delusion and the mind without delusion;
- the developed mind and the undeveloped mind;
- the cramped mind and the scattered mind;
- the surpassable and the unsurpassable mind;
- the freed mind and the bound mind; and
- the concentrated mind and the unconcentrated mind.

Without holding onto the desired ones or resenting the undesirable ones, the state should just be clearly identified without any dejection or elation. When a certain mental state is present, it is simply described as a mental state and not as "I" or "mine."

The seemingly steady and solid mind turns out to be a stream of mental acts that come from nothing and go nowhere, continuing in a continuous sequence as thought progresses.

Fourth Foundation: Mindfulness of Dhammas

The practice of contemplating the dhammas is the final foundation of mindfulness. The term "dhammas" in this context refers to collections of phenomena arranged in a manner that reflects the purpose of the Buddha's teaching. These comprise components of enlightenment and hurdles to realization.

Chapter Three

DEALING WITH STRESS, ANXIETY, PANIC ATTACKS, AND DEPRESSION

"How can there be laughter, how can there be pleasure, when the whole world is burning? When you are in deep darkness, will you not ask for a lamp?" - Buddha

When most people hear the word meditation, they probably picture a person sitting still with their legs crossed in a serene environment. But there are many ways to meditate, and while it does take some effort to get the hang of it, even a few minutes a day can help lessen the symptoms of common mental health issues like anxiety and depression.

According to research, meditation can reduce stress hormones, enhance focus, improve sleep, and lessen physical pain. Additionally, meditation helps in changing the body's molecular neurotransmitters that could be causing depression and anxiety.

Even if it all seems wonderful on paper, it's normal to be apprehensive about beginning a meditation routine for depression or anxiety. Fortunately, it's easier than you would imagine—and evidence suggests it's well worth the effort.

An Overview of Stress Management

Stress management is methods, plans, and treatments used to help people control their stress. This may involve reducing acute stress, but it often aims to reduce chronic stress in order to enhance general health, pleasure, and well-being. Some examples of stress-reduction techniques include deep breathing, eating a nutritious diet, getting adequate sleep, guided visualization, hobbies and pastimes, meditation, mindfulness, positive thinking, progressive muscle relaxation, psychotherapy, social support, and yoga.

Stress is a part of everyone's daily existence. Understanding how it affects your body and mastering effective stress management techniques are crucial if you want stress to work for you rather than against you, as many health issues are either caused by or influenced by stress.

Stress: what is it?

Stress is your body's reaction to changes in your life. There is no way to avoid stress because life is full of constant change, from minor adjustments like commuting from home to work to large ones like getting married, divorcing, or losing a loved one.

Instead of trying to get rid of all stress, your goal should be to get rid of the stress that is unneeded and handle the remainder well. Although there are some common sources of stress that many individuals encounter, every individual is unique.

Causes of stress

There are several potential "stressors" that can cause stress. Because our perceptions of what we encounter in life (based on our individual combinations of personality traits, resources, and habitual thought patterns) determine what we experience as "stressful," a situation may be "stressful" to one person but merely "challenging" to another.

Simply said, what triggers stress for one person may not be distressing for another. However, some circumstances can make people more susceptible to stress and burnout than others.

For instance, we are more prone to feel stressed when we are faced with demanding circumstances but have limited control and few options. Stress can also arise when we lack the necessary skills when we fear harsh judgment from others, and when the penalties for failing are severe or uncertain.

Numerous factors, including more banal ones like clutter or busy schedules, as well as individuals' employment, relationships, financial difficulties, and health concerns, cause stress in many people. Your experience of stress can be lessened by developing coping mechanisms for dealing with various stressors.

Effects

There are many ways that stress can affect your health and well-being. It can make it more difficult to handle life's minor inconveniences, have a negative impact on your interpersonal connections, and harm your health. It becomes clear that your mind and body are connected when you consider how stress affects your life.

Physical health problems might result from feeling anxious about a relationship, money, or living condition. The opposite is also true. Health issues, such as diabetes or high blood pressure, can have an impact on how stressed out you are and how you feel about yourself. When your brain is under a lot of stress, your body responds as a result.

Heart attacks, arrhythmias, and even sudden death can result from severe or acute stress, which can be brought on by situations like becoming caught up in a natural disaster or getting into a verbal dispute. However, people with existing chronic cardiac disease may be more likely to experience this.

Stress also causes emotional damage. While moderate stress may cause mild worry or annoyance, prolonged stress can also cause depression, anxiety disorders, and burnout.

Prolonged stress can take a toll on your health. When faced with ongoing stress, your autonomic nervous system will be overactive, which could harm your health.

Diabetes, hair loss, heart disease, hyperthyroidism, obesity, sexual dysfunction, tooth and gum disease, and ulcers—all of these disorders are influenced by stress.

Consult your doctor if you notice any physical symptoms that you believe may be caused by stress to make sure you are taking the best possible measures to protect your health. Stress-related symptoms should not be dismissed as "all in your head" and should instead be addressed seriously.

Five Ways Meditation Can Help You Manage and Reduce Stress

Let's examine some of the specific ways that meditation can help in stress management and the promotion of better health and well-being.

1. Meditation reverses the impacts of the stress response

During meditation, you transition from a state of activity to one of silence. You navigate through the stream of thoughts in your mind and arrive at a condition of peaceful attention. Although you are deeply at rest, your mind is awake and vigilant. In this relaxed state, there are a number of restorative impacts on the body that are the antithesis of the fight-or-flight reaction, including:

- Blood pressure is returned to normal.
- Heart rate is reduced.
- Stress hormones like cortisol and adrenaline are produced less often.
- The immune system is strengthened.
- The body uses oxygen more effectively.
- Deeper breathing.
- There is less inflammation overall.

2. Meditation increases the body's wellbeing-inducing neurotransmitters

Meditation induces a profound level of relaxation that causes the brain to release neurotransmitters that improve mood, focus, and inner tranquility. The following are some of the important neurotransmitters that are released during meditation:

- Dopamine
- Serotonin
- GABA (gamma-aminobutyric acid)
- Endorphins

No one medicine can orchestrate the simultaneous release of these neurotransmitters like meditation does, and it does so without any negative side effects.

3. Meditation encourages calm and restful sleep

The persistent lack of sleep that many of us experience raise our stress levels and irritability. According to scientific research, meditation can help you achieve the peaceful sleep you need for your physical and mental well-being. It is also an effective treatment for insomnia.

4. Focus and attention are improved by meditation

Many people experience stress as a result of juggling multiple tasks at once. Neuroscientists have found that the conscious brain is incapable of multitasking. For instance, if I engage in a conversation with you while simultaneously checking my emails, I'm doing neither. Instead of allowing your attention to be diverted by every passing idea and distraction, meditation helps you educate your brain to stay focused on the work at hand. You become more productive and less anxious when you focus on a particular thing at a time.

5. Emotional turbulence is released through meditation

By practicing meditation, you can observe your thoughts, feelings, and stories with more objectivity and distance, which helps you build "witnessing awareness," preventing you from getting sucked into the melodrama of emotional reactivity. The inner agitation naturally calms when you start to observe your mental activity without seeking to change it or reject it. You will eventually start to notice that challenging emotional states have some space surrounding them. You may also notice that the sensations connected to the negative state completely vanish when you begin to understand that there is more to who you are than your feelings or thoughts.

How to Manage Anxiety and Panic Attacks with Meditation

Anyone who has anxiety or has experienced a panic attack will tell you that feeling confined is one of the worst elements of the experience. It can seem as though there is no way to make the feelings go away or that there is no hope of relief as the waves of worry sweep over you. You wonder if you'll ever feel normal or in control again.

All panic attacks or anxiety will end eventually. In some ways, you just have to ride out the waves until it passes. However, there are strategies to control anxieties and panic attacks so they end more quickly and even ways to prevent them from starting in the first place.

Meditation is one of the most effective ways to deal with anxiety and panic attacks. Numerous research has indicated that practicing meditation can help people feel less stressed and anxious.

Don't worry; you don't need to be an "expert" at meditation to benefit from it. According to research, people who have anxiety can start to feel better even after a one-hour introduction to meditation.

Let's examine the benefits of meditation for reducing anxiety and panic attacks, as well as some simple suggestions for getting started with meditation for this purpose.

Signs of anxiety and panic attacks

Most of us have had a panic attack at some point in our lives, usually when we were under a lot of stress. About one in every 75 individuals has panic disorder. The fact that a panic attack often feels as though it comes out of nowhere is one of its most terrifying aspects. People who have panic attacks may feel entirely normal one minute and then suddenly feel extremely anxious.

Individuals with anxiety and panic attacks will experience them in different ways, but a panic attack will always involve the following symptoms:

- A pounding heartbeat
- Difficult breathing
- Anxious, rushing thoughts
- Sensing a sense of impending dread or terror
- Feeling as if you're going to pass out
- Sensing as though you're "going crazy"
- Shaking and sweating
- Constipation and other digestive issues
- Experiencing nausea or vertigo

How Does Meditation Help Those Suffering from Anxiety and Panic Attacks?

According to experts, the body's fight or flight reactions are responsible for the symptoms of a panic attack. Hormones like cortisol and adrenaline are released during this response, tricking the body into believing it is in danger even though it is not.

Meditation can help people with panic attacks by causing their bodies to go into relaxation mode. It gives the body the impression that it is safe through various practices like mindfulness, breathing, visualization, and grounding oneself in the present.

You can improve your awareness of the present moment and learn to let go of anxious thoughts by practicing mindfulness and meditation.

Meditation can be used as a preventative measure by those who often have panic attacks as a vital component of their normal wellness regimen. By being able to recognize the beginning of an episode and respond appropriately, they can reduce the likelihood that it will happen in the first place.

How Meditation Helps with Depression

Depression is a complicated mental health condition that results in low mood and may make a person feel hopeless or sad much of the time.

Age-related depression is still a serious health concern for older people. Regular depression can increase the risk of heart disease and illness-related death. It affects 20% of people over the age of 65. Additionally, it has an impact on people's daily life by increasing social isolation and impairing cognitive performance, particularly memory.

In response to loss or tragedy, depressive symptoms may appear briefly. However, if the symptoms persist for more than two weeks, it may indicate a significant depressive condition.

In fact, a study discovered that people with more severe depressive symptoms also had poorer episodic memory or the capacity to recall certain experiences and events.

Depression can be treated in a variety of ways. The standard first-line therapies for depression are antidepressants and psychotherapy; however, current research indicates that regular meditation practice may benefit by changing how the brain reacts to stress and anxiety.

If you have depression, you may experience persistent symptoms, including a persistently depressed mood. Alternatively, you can have major depression several times a year. Additionally, over time, you might see your symptoms varying or getting worse.

Treatments for depression can sometimes be quite effective right away. You might:

- Locate a good therapist
- Benefit from short or medium-term medication
- Change your way of life, where possible, to alleviate symptoms

The general treatment for depression is antidepressant drugs, either alone or in conjunction with psychotherapy. While they are typically advised and often employed as the first-line strategy for treating depression, it is often possible to improve the results by combining conventional therapies with natural alternatives.

Meditation is one such all-natural treatment. You can often feel better through meditation, change your thoughts and behaviors, and control your depressive symptoms more quickly.

Below is an outline of how meditation may be beneficial when practiced alongside the above treatments.

How does meditation help?

It's completely understandable if you harbor some skepticism about the idea. You might even relate it with advice commonly given by people who suggest that by simply smiling more and adopting a positive mindset your depression will miraculously improve.

Although meditation alone won't make your symptoms go away, it can help you control them.

How? Read on.

It helps you change your reaction to negative thinking:

Depression brings about dark thoughts. You could feel helpless, unworthy, or even furious with yourself or your life. Due to the fact that meditation requires raising awareness of one's thoughts and feelings, it may appear somewhat counterintuitive.

However, meditation teaches you to be present with your feelings and thoughts without judging them or yourself.

Pushing these thoughts aside or acting as though you don't have them is not a part of meditation. Instead, you observe them, accept them, and then let them go. In this approach, meditation can help in severing undesirable thought patterns.

Let's say you and your partner are enjoying a peaceful moment. You experience joy and love. Then have the thought, "They're going to leave me."

Meditation can help you in reaching a state of:

- Taking note of the thought
- Recognize it as a potential outcome
- Recognize that it's not the only option

Meditation can help you in letting this thought pass through your consciousness and moving on, as opposed to responding to it with something like, "I'm not worthy of a good relationship."

It teaches you more effective methods for controlling depression:

Being mindful of the current moment can help you spot early depressive episode warning symptoms.

Meditation makes it easy to pay attention to your emotions as they come up. Therefore, you can decide to concentrate on self-care to prevent things from getting worse when you start to experience negative thought patterns or observe greater irritability, exhaustion, or decreased interest in the things you usually enjoy doing.

Additionally, promising research supports meditation:

Research suggests that mindfulness-based cognitive therapy, a type of psychotherapy that integrates mindfulness meditation techniques, can lessen your risk of relapsing into depression.

According to studies, when meditation techniques are continued in daily life, depression symptoms may be reduced. In other words, it can be more advantageous as a regular practice than a quick remedy.

You've probably heard that exercise might lessen the symptoms of depression. There is data to back up that conclusion, but a 2017 study of 181 nursing students showed that meditation might be even more effective at treating depression.

Chapter Four

HOW TO BRING MINDFULNESS INTO YOUR LIFE

"Loss of mindfulness is why people engage in useless pursuits, do not care for their own interests, and remain unalarmed in the presence of things which actually menace their welfare." – Buddha

Have you ever found yourself eating an ice cream cone, took a few licks, and suddenly realized all you had in your hand was a sticky napkin? Or perhaps you've been going somewhere and arrived at your destination only to discover you haven't noticed anyone or anything you met along the way? Of course, it happens! These are typical instances of "mindlessness," or, as some could say, "going on automatic pilot." Which can make you question, "How can I incorporate more mindfulness into my daily life?"

We all develop mental and physical habits, as well as attention and inattention patterns, which prevent us from being fully present in our own lives. This inattention might have expensive repercussions. They can cause us to lose out on some really great opportunities as well as some crucial signals and information about our lives, our relationships, and even our own health.

Mindfulness starts to get intriguing when we can learn to incorporate it into daily life. Mindfulness, as you may know, refers to being in the present moment. If you can do it while sitting in a chair, why not do it while doing other things like shopping, drinking tea, eating, holding a baby, using the computer, or having conversations with friends? These are all chances to practice mindfulness and awareness.

Making mindfulness a regular part of your life can be healthy for both your mind and body. Integrating it into your everyday life doesn't have to be hard, and it can be as simple as practicing daily mindful breathing exercises.

What is Mindfulness?

As basic as it may sound, mindfulness is a quality and skill that anyone can acquire and use on a daily basis. According to Deepak Chopra, mindfulness means being aware of your surroundings and being in the present. Whatever you are doing, you can practice mindfulness, and it doesn't take up any additional time in your day. Mindfulness involves utilizing all of your senses to remain in the present moment. You keep your attention on what you are doing rather than dwelling on the past or fretting about the future.

Put simply, mindfulness is the ability to observe the present moment without passing judgment. It serves as a valuable tool for countering negative thoughts. Mindfulness means returning yourself to the present and simply paying attention to what is happening at that moment, rather than projecting into the future and envisioning worst-case scenarios. For individuals who are still exploring different techniques to manage their stress or anxiety, starting with mindfulness practice is often the easiest place to start. Constant meditation can also lead to greater levels of mindfulness.

How Mindfulness Differs from Meditation

The internet is flooded with the benefits of mindfulness and meditation. Both terms are often used interchangeably with little clarification.

This can be perplexing for people who want to begin meditating or living mindfully from scratch.

Although they are connected, mindfulness and meditation are not the same. You can create a practice that suits your needs if you have a fundamental understanding of how these two ideas differ from one another.

There are numerous varieties of meditation, each with unique characteristics and techniques that guide the practitioner in various paths for self-development. Knowing one's goals and the benefits that each style of meditation offers is necessary before choosing a practice.

Here, we deconstruct mindfulness and go over the parallels and divergences of mindful meditation. This section is created to provide clarity in order for you to start or continue the journey toward your individual mindfulness and meditation goals.

Before we start this exploration, it is helpful to look at some definitions of the two constructs.

1. Meditation is a practice; mindfulness is a quality

Consider the following researcher's definition of meditation: Meditation is a practice where one adopts a technique – like mindfulness or concentrating the mind on a specific object, thought, or activity - to train attention and awareness and reach a mentally clear, emotionally peaceful, and stable state.

In contrast, mindfulness is the awareness that develops as a result of paying intentional attention to the present moment without passing judgment.

While meditation is described as a disciplined practice aiming to change or strengthen one's state of mind, mindfulness is defined as a way of responding to oneself and one's environment.

Despite the fact that each notion has a wide range of definitions, these two clearly differ from one another. Mindfulness is one of the qualities that can be developed through the practice of meditation.

There is a category of meditation techniques known as "mindfulness meditation," which helps the practitioner in acting and living mindfully. As we shall see, however, there are other types of meditative practice, of which mindfulness meditation is only one.

2. Meditation is one of the various paths to mindful living

One way to practice living in the moment is through meditation. We can also see meditation as a method for mastering mindfulness.

People who want to be more mindful in their daily experiences can benefit greatly from meditation. For instance, people who regularly and methodically practice mindfulness meditation, such as those who take part in the MBSR program, are better able to act mindfully in daily situations.

The seeds of mindfulness can be planted during meditation and nurtured over the course of our life.

Although highly beneficial for this goal, meditation is only one method of developing mindfulness, as we will discover later.

3. Mindfulness can be used in treatment without incorporating meditation

The quality of mindfulness has been linked to numerous advantages for mental health as well as other positive traits like self-worth and self-acceptance.

For these reasons, many professionals believe that helping their clients live mindfully is worthwhile. However, not every client is open to meditation or prepared to incorporate a structured practice into their daily lives.

Dialectical Behavior Therapy (DBT) is a good example of a therapy that uses mindfulness to benefit patients without mandating formal meditation. DBT is designed to help clients acquire a "wise mind" by teaching them various skills that enable them to exhibit the characteristics of mindfulness. Without ever requiring them to engage in formal practice, DBT clinicians help their clients develop a mindfulness practice.

4. Both formal and informal practices of mindfulness exist

It is counterintuitive to meditate because it is a practice of "non-doing." Generally speaking, the task is to learn to see one's inner world by making little effort and adopting a non-judgmental attitude.

These characteristics go against the way that many of us conduct our lives—striving for advancement and putting work before rest. Formal meditation, which involves sitting for a set amount of time, can help us escape the hustle and bustle of everyday life and serve as a gentle reminder that we don't necessarily need to work so hard to attain our objectives or be the people we want to be.

Not everyone wants to practice formal mindfulness, despite its many benefits. However, they may still desire to live more mindfully. Fortunately, mindfulness may be practiced in a variety of informal contexts, including mindful walking, mindful eating, and even mindful conversation. To informally practice mindfulness is to go about one's daily business with awareness in mind.

This entails taking your time, being present, putting your judgment aside, and giving your all to whatever experience is taking place in the present moment.

5. Mindfulness is just one component of meditation

Although mindfulness is a crucial component of meditation, there are other elements that make it unique.

Concentration is another essential component of meditation. The mind is prone to wandering to a myriad of unexpected areas when it isn't being stimulated by outside factors, such as while practicing formal meditation. It is challenging to stay focused on the current meditation practice while the mind is straying.

Training your attention to focus more intently enables more fruitful and successful meditation, as well as perhaps more mindfulness in daily life.

Following the discussion about how these two practices differ from one another, meditation is essentially a broad phrase that refers to the practice of developing strength and awareness to notice and modify the mental state. Mercy, patience, and mindfulness are just a few of the traits and techniques that must manifest through a more developed mental state.

However, just like yoga, mindfulness falls under the umbrella of meditation. Meditation does not involve shutting off the mind, nor does mindfulness include stressing and intense thought.

Both of these techniques are skills that enable us to embrace inner and outer peace. They offer ways to find happiness and decrease suffering by letting go of fears about the past and the future.

How Mindfulness Also Forms One of the Meditation Techniques – Mindful Meditation

Mindful meditation is a mental exercise that teaches you to quiet your body and mind, let go of negativity, and slow down your racing thoughts. It blends meditation with mindfulness, which is a mental state that entails being totally present in "the now" in order to accept and appreciate your thoughts, feelings, and sensations without condemnation.

Although methods might differ, mindfulness meditation often entails deep breathing and awareness of one's body and mind. There is no need for props when practicing mindfulness meditation (unless you like using mantras, candles, or essential oils). All you need to get started is a relaxed spot to sit, ten minutes of free time, and a mindset free of judgment.

Tips to Practice Mindfulness in Daily Life

Bringing mindful, non-judgmental awareness to the present moment has received a lot of attention lately;

formerly considered to be only a spiritual practice, it is becoming more common in the workplace and in popular culture. According to research, people are much happier when they are paying attention to what they are doing than when they are thinking about something enjoyable.

While creating a meditation practice is the quickest approach to acquiring a strong degree of mindfulness in your life, the ultimate goal is to incorporate it into daily living—to experience longer and longer stretches of clear, tranquil attention to the present moment. Fortunately, there are several opportunities throughout each day to focus on the present moment; all it takes is willpower. These seven suggestions are just that—places to start. Once you understand it, you can use mindfulness at any time to observe how your experience is changed.

1. Mindful eating

No matter the plans you have for the day, it's inevitable that you'll have meals to enjoy, at the very least, some snacks. An excellent technique to incorporate mindfulness into your day is to remind yourself to return to the present moment each time you eat. This will also make you more aware of the foods you're putting into your body.

Pay close attention to aromas, textures, and tastes - every mouthful of food has a lot to be noticed. Even a small raisin can make you happy if you're truly paying attention! Take small bites and chew slowly, relishing as you go - wait until you have finished swallowing before picking up your fork to take the next bite.

2. Mindful waking

Instead of slamming your palm on the alarm clock and jumping out of bed in the morning, setting an intention to bring mindfulness into the opening minutes of your day is a nice, calm way to set the tone for hours to come. Pay close attention to your body and thoughts. Do you feel rested or alert? Do your muscles feel tense? Slowly extend your arms, legs, and back, paying attention to how each movement feels. Try to pay attention to the thoughts that come to mind as soon as you open your eyes or even just before.

3. Mindful cleaning

Whether it's folding laundry, cleaning the floor, or doing the dishes, chores offer a great chance to practice mindfulness. In fact, outside of scheduled sitting times, the majority of meditation retreats encourage students to keep up their practice by assigning them to such activities.

Pay close attention to whatever your hands are doing. When washing dishes, pay attention to the water's temperature, the plates' texture, and the scrubbing action. Feel the various fabrics when folding laundry. As you sweep, pay attention to how your arms move, how they stretch and extend, and whether they start to hurt after a while.

4. Mindful showering

While it is true that we often have our finest ideas when in the shower, showering may also be a time to take a break from the constant stream of thoughts that occupies most of the day and focus on being present.

Focus on how the water feels. Take note of the temperature before and after you adjust, the sensation of each drop as it touches your skin, and the sound it makes when it hits the shower curtain, screen, or tiles.

5. Mindful walking

Just like eating, every day includes some walking, whether it's a long stroll to work or school or a short one to the kitchen. Every step offers the opportunity to practice mindfulness.

Pay close attention to how your legs and feet feel. How each foot strikes the ground, rolls, and then pushes off once more. As you advance, notice how each leg bends and how your calf and thigh muscles are stretched. As you focus more intently, you can also become aware of your hip joints rotating, your arms swinging, the alignment of your spine, and the breeze on your face.

6. Mindful waiting

When you first see the long queue at the bank, you might sigh, but practicing mindfulness as you wait might change that sigh into a real smile. Being forced to wait gives us a chance to experience emotional reactions quickly and strongly; therefore, it's also an opportunity to pay attention to both your mind and your body.

Pay close attention to the entire experience. If you have to wait, pay attention to how you feel. Does your heart beat faster? Are you irritated? Angry? Your fists might even clench automatically. Are you breathing differently? Whilst you are sitting or standing in the queue or at the bus stop, pull your focus away from the cerebral and emotional aspects of your experience and pay attention to your body. Feel your breathing in and out and your feet on the ground. Take note of every single small movement.

7. Mindful working

While working, you have the opportunity to cultivate mindfulness. The work environment can make it easy to become stressed out. By employing mindfulness, you can anchor your attention to each task at hand, preventing yourself from slipping into that trap. Let's assume you are struggling with a spreadsheet. This presents a chance to practice mindfulness. Break the process down into manageable parts while focusing on the computer screen. Take a look at just one cell in the spreadsheet you're using. Pay attention to one row at a time. You will be able to do better work if you are mindful while working.

When you have to go to business meetings, you can also practice mindfulness. Meetings may be intimidating, whether they take place in a boardroom or online. Here is where mindfulness can be of assistance. Focus on the meeting participant who is speaking. As you listen, pay attention to your feelings. It is possible to hold negative feelings towards meetings or experience anxiety in relation to them. You might dislike meetings or get frustrated by them, or perhaps you're disappointed because you're not getting a promotion or credit. All of these are chances to cultivate mindfulness.

8. Mindful listening

You know that cathartic feeling you get after having a long, intimate chat with a friend when you truly feel like you've let something out? Unaware of it, your friend was probably engaging in mindful listening. One of the finest ways to connect and strengthen our relationships, both at home and at work, is by truly being with those who are close to us.

Pay close attention to not just the words being spoken to you but everything about the person speaking. Naturally, listen to them, but also pay close attention to their body language. Avoid the temptation to begin planning your next words before the other person has finished speaking; instead, simply listen.

Chapter Five

HOW TO START
MEDITATING: THE BASICS

*"Meditation brings wisdom; lack of
meditation leaves ignorance. Know well
what leads you forward and what holds you
back, and choose the path that leads to
wisdom." —Buddha*

In our fast-paced environment, we can often
encounter a barrage of noise and distractions. It is
common to find ourselves pulled away from the
present moment, as our focus and attention and
drawn to other matters, whether or not they hold
true importance in that particular instance. This can
lead to feelings of tension, anxiety, or a sense of
losing control.

*"The horse is galloping quickly, and it appears that
the rider on the horse is going somewhere
important. Another man, standing alongside the*

road, shouts, 'Where are you going?' and the horse rider replies, 'I don't know! Ask the horse!'"

This quote from an old Buddhist parable perfectly captures a state of mind for a lot of people. Consider yourself the rider, the horse your life, and you are allowing it to gallop without knowing where it is going or actively leading it to a destination of your choice.

You can stop the horse from rushing along a route beyond your control and begin to exert some control and direction by meditating and beginning to live mindfully, becoming more aware of the present, of choices you can make and the paths you wish to follow.

Once you achieve that stillness, you can direct your mind to focus on important things: the people you love, the task at hand, and what is truly important to you. You will see a significant improvement in the quality of your life and peace of mind.

In this chapter, we'll explore the fundamentals of meditation and how to get started. I'll cover important aspects such as preparation, posture, breathing and cultivating focused attention. I will also share valuable tips on establishing a regular meditation routine.

Through the practice of meditation, we have the opportunity to reconnect with our inner selves and the present moment. By calmly sitting and observing our thoughts without judgement, we gain insights into the workings of our minds. This process allows us to recognize patterns of thought and emotion that may be limiting us, empowering us to cultivate new perspectives, ways of thinking and being.

Learning to meditate is a process and developing a consistent meditation practice requires time and patience. Nonetheless, the advantages are worthwhile. We can discover inner peace, clarity, and direction. We may reconnect with our true selves and live more fully in the moment. So, let us begin our meditation adventure and begin taming the wild galloping horse.

Preparing for Meditation to get the most from it

You don't necessarily need any tools or equipment to practice meditation. You can meditate while riding the subway, sleeping, or even bathing! Simply take a deep breath in and see yourself doing so. Exhale and be aware of it as you are doing so. That's it. You're meditating! Simply sit with your breath, and your whole attention focused on it.

However, your meditative experience can be immensely improved by making yourself physically, mentally, and spiritually ready.

I have compiled a checklist to help you carve out time and prepare for your practice so you can be more successful. Using some or all of the suggestions, you can develop a mindful pre-meditation routine that will swiftly prepare your mind and body for focus and attention. Use any or all of these to achieve the most out of your meditation session.

Consult Your Doctor

Speak with your healthcare professional if you have any concerns about engaging in your meditation. Most medical professionals know the many therapeutic benefits of meditation and can advise you. They'll likely support and reassure you in your endeavor.

Find Ways to Carve Out Time in Your Busy Day

How do you know when is the optimum moment to meditate? It's natural to sometimes lack the motivation to meditate due to other responsibilities. Meditation must be a scheduled activity that you commit to in order to be effective, rather than something you do whenever you feel like it. Dealing with your normal responsibilities and obligations, on the other hand, can be more beneficial than meditating during the day because you are removing items from your mental landscape that would otherwise interrupt your peace of mind. Then there's life's inescapable business: children, spouse, classes, meetings, and the like, which does not count as a distraction. Here are six pointers to help you make time in your hectic day:

1. Make a schedule for when you will meditate

Meditation on a set schedule might feel archaic, type-A, or anal-retentive. However, scheduling anything denotes its significance. Writing things down, especially putting them on paper, has a huge impact on memory. You make a commitment to yourself by writing down your meditation appointment. Furthermore, you are telling yourself that you value your health enough to make time for yourself every day.

2. Pick a time when there are few distractions

The most effective time to meditate is in the morning, as it allows you to dedicate uninterrupted time to your practice without needing to take a break from work or getting caught up in the busyness of the day. Evenings can be another favorable time for meditation, particularly when you have completed your daily tasks and activities, providing a sense of closure and allowing for a peaceful transition into relaxation and introspection. Utilize these two windows if you can.

3. Look for little gaps in your schedule

Putting on the most frantic performance possible appears to be a cultural need. But the average day is more like Swiss cheese than a solid wall of activity. The idea is to look for the small pockets of air where you may have some alone time. Remember that we are only talking about a short period. Most people don't have the luxury of large blocks of time, but almost everyone can find smaller periods of 10 to 20 minutes.

4. Stick to your scheduled meditation time

Once you've identified your meditation time, schedule and write it down. Set an alert on your smartphone if that helps. When it's time, put everything on hold to begin your meditation. Be aware that some things will happen which will tempt you to stray from your plan. You'll get a call, a deadline will change, and your email and social media outlets will ping.

5. Take only necessary breaks

Identify the difference between the emergency that requires your immediate attention and the typical noise haze you can avoid. You may have problems telling noise from an emergency. Ask yourself, "Can this wait for a few minutes? If I don't take care of this immediately, will someone suffer; will my work or reputation suffer?" Reassure yourself that you can return to whatever problem arose as soon as the meditation is done. After meditating, you may feel more in control of the situation than before.

6. Meditate anyway

Even if you still find it difficult to let go, try meditating anyway. It is preferable to meditate despite being distracted as opposed to not meditating at all. Don't worry if you miss a session because you must continue working; just pick up where you left off at the next scheduled time. But don't feel obligated to extend a session to make up for your missed sessions; guilt-tripping yourself is counterproductive. This is about your evolving development, not some fictitious barometer of perfection.

Develop a Consistent Routine

One of the most often asked questions is about making meditation practice consistent. Set aside a certain time for practice and stick to it as strictly as possible. This should be the best answer to your question. But first, why should you bring regular consistency to your meditation?

- Regular meditation practice broadens your awareness and consciousness. Meditation is an attempt to clear your mind of negative thoughts. You can't cast them out unless you're consistent.

- When you meditate, you can connect with wonderful thoughts or visions. But if you don't feed them regularly, they will start to fade.

- Regular meditation helps you establish subjective connections with higher forces. You can eventually function at higher levels where creative forces sit by regularly practicing meditation. Rhythm and harmony are magnets for the creative forces. There are creative energies around, which cultivate more inspiration.

- Regular meditation helps discipline your body, nervous system, heart, and brain. It trains your emotional body, and it sharpens, concentrates, awakens, and inspires your mental body. The old habits of your body reappear after you go a few days without practicing meditation.

- Regular meditation keeps your mind from wandering while you concentrate, focus, analyze, and synthesize. The mind is trained by consistent and regular action.

With this background, let's discuss some helpful tips for making meditation a regular practice.

1. Convince yourself that you deserve your self-realization. The more deeply we meditate, the more our brain gets rewired to experience subtle reality.
2. You are allowed to skip a day of practice for whatever reason. Don't feel bad about it. However, don't come up with ridiculous reasons for avoiding or skipping practice.
3. The brain becomes bored. So, experiment with various meditation techniques.
4. Meditation doesn't necessitate giving up the material world, traveling to the Himalayas, or enrolling on a pricey course.
5. Be kind to yourself. Don't be hard on yourself for past mistakes. The fact that you missed a few meditation sessions shouldn't stop you from meditating again.

To bring consistency to your meditation, you can begin with 3 to 4 times a week and build on this until it becomes a daily habit. Ideally, at the same time of day, which will help build a habit.

Start with a Short Time

People often express their frustration at not being able to shift from not meditating to consistently meditating, despite wanting to establish a mindfulness meditation practice. Others merely lack the time in their schedules. Making new habits or taking the time to sit down and be present for 20, 40 or 60 minutes can be challenging. I suggest you start small. Really small. Start with just 5 minutes a day for the first week if you're new to meditation. Find a time that will consistently work for you, whether right after getting out of bed but before beginning the day, during a midday break, or right before bed.

It shouldn't be too difficult to find 5 minutes, but if your ultimate goal is to build a deeper practice, you should think about creating a plan that will allow for extended stretches in the future.

During the first week, set your smartphone's stopwatch for 5 minutes daily at around the same time. I suggest you make sure the alarm tone is a light non-jarring one, set on a low volume. You will be sitting in silence so that should be sufficient to hear it without being shocked out of your meditational space - that would be counter-productive to what you are trying to achieve. Prepare and settle yourself before beginning, and focus entirely during that period.

The next week, continue your meditation at the same time of day while timing it for 10 minutes with a stopwatch. Add 5 minutes each subsequent week until you reach the span of time that feels ideal for you. While some prefer hour-long sessions, others can manage 10 or 15 minutes. There is no perfect way to meditate, and there is no ideal duration. If you can only spare 5 or 10 minutes, use them wisely. The goal is to strengthen your ability to focus on being more present during the rest of your waking hours.

I didn't come up with this strategy. Many behavioral scientists have discovered that taking small steps is the best way to accomplish big goals. Therefore, if you want to develop other habits, set a big goal—for example, "I'd like to read more books"—and then break it down into smaller goals. For example, "I'll start by reading one page each night before I go to bed for the first two weeks, and then read three pages the following week." These actions, consistently taken, develop into new habits after a few months.

Make Sure You're Not Hungry

Since the beginning of meditation practice, one question has persisted in the minds of practitioners: When is the ideal time to meditate? Before eating, after eating, or while eating?

Let's examine the common benefits and drawbacks of practicing meditation on an empty stomach to understand how food affects the intensity or outcomes of meditation.

The benefits of meditating on an empty stomach include:

- Your mind is alert on an empty stomach, which facilitates the development of a more advanced meditative state.

- A focused meditative state is facilitated by an empty stomach, which also enhances cognitive function.
- If you practice mindful meditation, a little hunger can help you reach a more intense meditative experience since it enhances your emotional capabilities.
- Studies have revealed that the hormone ghrelin, which causes the sensation of hunger, has a substantial impact on the hippocampus, the area of the brain in charge of learning and memory. Therefore, meditating on an empty stomach can benefit your brain's learning and memory processes.
- An empty stomach facilitates mindful, emotion-based, and focus-based meditations.
- Due to evolutionary tendencies, when you are hungry, your mind becomes attentive. At the same time, your senses are acute and focused, helping you connect with your deeper self and the body.
- Due to increased tranquility and attention after finishing your meditation on an empty stomach, you have a greater sensory perception of the food's flavor, smell, and texture when you finally eat. As a result, you feel profound gratitude and satisfaction.

The drawbacks of practicing meditation on an empty stomach include:

- Our emotions can become a little more erratic when we are hungry, and if we try to practice meditation when we are emotionally agitated, it might not be a pleasant experience.
- If you have been hungry for a long time and sit for meditation, your hunger pangs can become a distraction, leading to an unsatisfactory meditative state.
- We normally feel physically uncomfortable when hungry because it is our body's signal to replenish energy through eating. Being hungry might be a barrier when we must maintain a comfortable position while meditating.
- Make sure you're fully hydrated so you don't misread the signs of hunger.

After eating, it is advisable to wait at least 90 minutes to 2 hours before beginning a meditation session.

Our bodies direct energy and other resources toward the digestive system after a meal. As a result, our body lacks the sensory focus and awareness required for meditation during the following few hours. The body enters a condition of partial hibernation, where effective digestion of the food consumed becomes its top priority. This is why we often feel tired and dull after a substantial meal.

Wear Loose, Comfortable Clothing

Even without the possibility of being distracted by uncomfortable clothing, your mind, and thoughts can be distracting enough to dramatically reduce your chances of having a rewarding and meaningful meditation session.

There isn't any formal definition of what constitutes meditation clothes; instead, the term "meditation clothes" is used to describe a variety of good quality, comfortable clothing, ideally made of natural fibers, that won't interfere with your ability to focus while meditating.

How to choose to dress for meditation

- As a general rule, clothing for meditation should be breathable (cotton), soft, flexible, and eco-friendly (fair-trade or similar) fabrics.
- The size and flexibility of the clothing are other factors to consider. Ideally, you should strike a balance between fitted and loose clothing. It's preferable if they are neither tight nor loose in the middle.
- Consider color as a third factor when choosing clothing for meditation. Choose softer colors whenever possible, such as light

blue, pure white, soft green, Tuscan beige, or any combination of colors you like as long as they are easy on your eyes.

However, no specific clothing is required for meditation. Just aim to wear comfortable, focus-enhancing clothing.

Prepare Your Space and Remove Distractions

Our homes are a carefully managed collection of devoted rooms, so if you often meditate (or would like to), setting aside a space for it makes perfect sense.

It's easy to come up with justifications for not doing what we ought to do because we don't think we have the space or there are too many distractions, but creating a sanctuary, no matter how small, can motivate you to maintain your routine and provide peace to your soul each time you enter the space.

Although you can meditate anywhere, it does help to have a dedicated space in your house, especially if you are just starting.

Creating a tranquil, distraction-free space at home can be beneficial for settling the mind and maintaining attention. Additionally, if you regularly meditate in the same spot in your home, the space will start to radiate calming energy. By merely walking to your meditation mat, dedicated floor space or chair (before you even start your practice), you will notice that you begin to breathe deeper through association.

While there are no hard-and-fast guidelines for creating a meditation space at home, I will outline where to start. You don't need much; less is often more. Simply reflecting on what brings you a sense of comfort and peace can be a good place to start when designing your ideal meditation space.

If you are in the comfort of your own home, choose the space where you feel most relaxed and undisturbed.

Seven ways to create a meditation space in your home

It's not necessary to set aside an entire room for meditation, but it is preferable to choose a quiet place with little 'traffic,' such as your own bedroom or a spare room. Just make sure the area is clutter-free. If preventing this becomes difficult, think about putting up a folding screen - these can be bought quite inexpensively or even found in a thrift store.

Why not go for it and designate a whole room for your practice if you have a spare room? It might also serve as a place for reading, yoga, or handicraft.

Ideas for a meditation room are provided below:

1. Opt for soothing colors

It can be a very simple room with only a few furnishings made of natural materials like wicker, wood, and linen, and using colors in earthy tones and chalky whites. The floor could have a smooth finish extending throughout the room, and the walls purposefully left blank.

The meditation area could be "dressed" with, soft blankets, mattresses, and cushions before a session to create a cozy and calming atmosphere. If being seated on floor cushions is a problem for you, then a comfortable chair, with a straight back and low enough to allow your feet to be flat on the floor, is an option.

Think about the colors that make you feel safe and at ease. Many people will find that light, neutral colors are the most peaceful, yet darker colors may make others feel more enclosed, secure, and at ease.

2. Add comfortable furnishings

Large cushions, sheepskins, mats, and blankets are necessary because comfort is a focus. If putting things out permanently is impossible, keep them on display by storing them in a natural basket. Putting them in a cabinet could make them "out of sight, out of mind."

3. Create soft lighting

Consider the type of light that helps you feel most focused. As humans, light has a huge impact on our mood. Natural light is fantastic, and depending on your schedule, you might want to pick a location that faces the sun to take advantage of lovely dawn or sunset light.

You could also choose a room with curtains and use candles as your light source if you want softer soothing lighting. Just make sure they are not close to any fabrics or flammable materials. Candles, incense, aromatherapy oils, and smudge sticks bring new dimensions to your ritual and illuminate the room.

4. Add scent to your rituals

Burning some herbs can help to purify the environment, while essential oils in an oil burner, in particular, help to promote relaxation.

These modifications are an important stage in getting your mind ready. Your meditation setup will contain certain components that can be used in your practice.

When you do something ritualistic, like light a candle, spread out a mat, or burn some sage, it reminds you that you are about to sit motionlessly and focus inside. These minor preparations for meditation serve to prepare both your body and mind for the practice.

5. Connect with nature

A few plants will make the area more welcoming and help improve the air quality. They will also help you feel more connected to nature.

6. Make your meditation space unique

You can add items that you feel help to ground you in your practice to the room without succumbing to clutter. Crystals, mala beads, or a singing bowl are often used as meditation aids, but only add them to your space if they help you to connect inwardly. Mala beads are particularly useful when undertaking a mantra meditation, allowing you to keep track of the number of repetitions as you chant.

A singing bowl, when the stick is run around the inside rim of the bowl, emits a deep singing sound and a strong vibration also begins. This can be a powerful way to enter into your meditation. Gently striking the bowl on the outside gives a different sound, which can also be used for clearing your space of any negative energies, as part of your preparations.

7. Remove any distracting noises

If you live in a city or your home has a lot of background noise, playing calming music can help reduce distractions. Each person has various needs. Different people have varying sensitivity levels; some are more sensitive to visual distractions, others to noise, and others to kinesthetic sensations (body awareness).

In light of this, keep in mind that your meditation space is private, so follow your gut instinct as to what seems right for you.

Never be afraid to experiment until you achieve a state of tranquility and clarity that enables you to establish a close connection with yourself. Consider yourself, then project it into the space that will shelter and sustain your body and mind.

Commit to a Length of Time

As we have already discussed, the duration of your daily practice will depend on whether you are just beginning or are working up to an amount of time that suits your needs and availability. Here are a few additional hints regarding how often and for how long to meditate:

How much time should be spent meditating?

Clinical mindfulness therapies, like Mindfulness-Based Stress Reduction (MBSR), often advise 40–45 minutes of daily meditation practice. The Transcendental Meditation (TM) tradition often advises twenty minutes twice daily. Twenty-minute meditation sessions are also often advised in interventions based on the Relaxation Response. Monks and nuns in Tibetan monasteries have conducted shamata meditation (a breath-focused meditation) for 10 to 15 minutes at a time for centuries. This was done by the nuns and monks multiple times each day. However, these suggested numbers are not particularly magical.

In this manner, meditation seems comparable to physical activity. There is no ideal amount of time to exercise, just as there is no ideal duration for meditation. The duration of your practice, whether meditation or physical activity, should be long enough to challenge you but not so long that you become discouraged or worn out.

Making it a regular part of your day is more significant than how long you meditate. The amount of time you meditate should therefore be manageable for you. If you meditate for 90 minutes one day because you have the time, it won't help you much if you feel bad the rest of the week because you can't do it again.

Similar to how exercise works, if your schedule prevents you from doing your typical meditation, there seems to be a benefit in even a small amount. Take this as an example: Suppose you jog two miles every day. You're busy one day and can only walk a half-mile. Is this more advantageous than lounging on the couch? Yes. Will it be as beneficial to you as running two miles? It's improbable. Similarly, there doesn't seem to be a certain amount of time for meditation where, if you fall short, you're wasting your time.

Set a Timer; as long as it is Silent

Did you know that the original use for incense sticks was to act as a marker for a period of time in meditation practice? If you wish to keep away from devices, then this could be a good option for you.

Do you need to set a timer while you meditate?

You know the nagging thought that without a timer, you might not meditate for long enough or that you might overshoot and be late for other events of your day.

Perhaps you are traveling and meditating, and you are concerned that you will miss your stop. Depending on the situation, you can decide to either set a timer or not. Using a timer while meditating can be beneficial or detrimental, depending on the situation.

In this section, I'll go over some of the justifications for and against using a timer.

When is setting a timer for meditation beneficial?

You will invariably worry about the time if you have an appointment or must be somewhere very soon and fear that you will be late. Set a timer and then allow yourself to lose track of the time to avoid that preoccupation.

Similarly, if you want to meditate for a fixed period of time and discover that you are concentrating on it rather than letting go, setting a timer may be the best solution for you. If you keep meditating until the timer sounds, you can sit down to meditate, knowing that you'll stick to your scheduled session.

Setting a timer has another benefit when you want to train yourself to be able to gauge time without a timer. You might wish to set a timer for just a few minutes to train yourself to feel time pass rather than time it.

You can experiment with different meditation techniques. Explore both silent and musical meditation. Try meditating while keeping your eyes open, and practice with and without a timer.

Remember, you don't want to be startled out of your meditation by a loud alarm going off when you use a timer! Instead, pick a sound setting on low volume that will help you gently emerge from your state of focus.

When is setting a timer for meditation not beneficial?

It might go either way when you set a timer for your meditation. Sure, you won't have to worry about running late because you'll be on schedule, but it could also have the exact opposite effect.

When you set a timer, you could find yourself returning subliminally to the question, "When will the timer go off?" This could develop into a sense of waiting for the timer, which would cause you to become distracted and lower the effectiveness of your meditation.

If you're not cautious, it can also make meditation feel like a chore since you feel like you have to sit until the alarm says you're done.

As long as I know I have enough time, I like to sit without a timer. But if I'm concerned that I won't have enough time, the timer gives me confidence, and I'll set it for however much time I have.

Then I won't have the constant worry that I'll be running late for something and can focus on my meditation.

I prefer to sit without the timer, though, if I have enough time. And on occasion, I leave the timer going so that after I'm done, I can see how long I spent meditating. This enables me to judge the passage of time more accurately through feeling rather than by looking at the time.

The use of a timer should encourage letting go and allowing your thoughts to flow without connection to a specific worry, such as an upcoming appointment or the anticipation of the timer going off, as this is one of the fundamental goals of meditation.

In the end, it is both a personal and a situational question. Therefore, I advise trying both approaches: using the timer as a tool for letting go as well as taking it away to promote freedom and release from its use.

Release any Physical Tension

This may help if you get stiff from sitting without moving. The physical nature of meditation is evident to anyone who has tried to sit motionless during a meditation session. Stretching activities, yoga asanas, or practicing some tai chi movements, help the body become more flexible, stronger, and more resilient so that we can meditate for longer periods.

Stretching, twisting, and strengthening movements in asana also help to clear the pranic pathways in the body, preparing the subtle body, or pranic body, for meditation. Asana facilitates mental clarity and relaxation by releasing constrained pranic energy.

If yoga is not possible for you, gentle Tai Chi movements help to awaken the chi energy and these too have many benefits in meditation practice. If you're not familiar with the basic movements in Tai Chi, there are many good YouTube videos to help you carry out gentle stretching exercises. A third alternative is to do some simple stretching of your body, starting with your neck, shoulders, and arms, and moving to your chest, abdomen, back, glutes, and legs, before settling into your preferred meditation posture.

Refine Your Posture

A lot is said about proper posture for meditation, such as its potential to help connect you with a cosmic energy source, align your chakras, or improve the flow of kundalini energy through your spine.

But in reality, it's much simpler than that.

You need to sit comfortably but erect for good meditation posture. This enables your muscles to unwind properly, your lungs to expand, and your mind to be alert and focused.

The challenging thing is maintaining a straight posture while relaxing your body. So, here is a brief guide to help you improve your meditation posture and make the most of your practice.

What is meditation posture?

The ideal meditative position is the lotus position. You'll get more comfortable in your body and mind if you continuously practice sitting still for a little bit longer each day or each week.

First off, when we think about it, we often exaggerate or overdo our posture. When sitting upright for meditation, we don't want to strain because doing so can get uncomfortable after a while.

The body should be in a comfortable, upright seated position for meditation. This can be performed on the floor, a cushion, or a chair. The head is inclined forward, and the hands are relaxed and resting on the lap.

Proper meditation posture in a chair

When we think about those who meditate, we always picture them sitting cross-legged on the floor. This is the traditional meditation posture. This posture has historically been preferred for meditation mostly because few people had access to seats in the past.

You may have physical limitations that will not allow you to sit in a lotus position on a floor cushion, particularly if you are older and less flexible. In this case, a comfortable chair with a straight back is a good alternative. Using a chair is no less advantageous as long as you sit upright. It also doesn't call for a lot of flexibility and is easier on your knees and hips.

You can modify this position to meet your needs. Everybody has a unique body type, and some people are limited in how they can sit due to age, injuries or aches. When adjusting to your posture, make the necessary changes without sacrificing the factors that are important to a proper meditation posture. Remember to keep your body upright, as in the lotus position, so you can allow your breath to flow easily. Make sure your feet can stay comfortably flat on the floor throughout your meditation. You might also find it helpful to have a soft cushion under your feet.

Why is proper posture so crucial when meditating?

There are various reasons why learning and sustaining a healthy posture in meditation is crucial.

- **Prevents pain:** If your posture is overly stretched while you're sitting, you risk experiencing pain. Newcomers often go overboard, which can cause unnecessary pain.

- **Minimizes distraction:** Avoid letting your posture become a detraction during practice. Being aware of your posture will help you concentrate on the exercise itself.
- **Maintains alertness:** When your body and posture are too relaxed, your mind may also become relaxed. While this isn't necessarily a bad thing, if you find it difficult to remain alert or even awake during meditation, the issue is probably with your posture.
- **Allows for long meditation sessions:** Longer meditation sessions are possible when you have proper posture while meditating since you can hold that position for a longer period.

Adjust Your Breath

The goal of practicing meditation is to develop awareness and peace, yet new practitioners frequently lose focus by obsessing over their breathing. They wonder if there is a "right way" to breathe during meditation. Typical worries include: Should I breathe as usual? Do I breathe in and out through my mouth or my nose? Which should be filled with air, my tummy or my lungs?

Most meditation professionals advise letting your body breathe normally. Just allow your breathing to be shallow if it is and deep if it is. Some encourage you to start with several deep breaths as an optional exercise.

It's possible to inhale through your nose and exhale from your mouth. You can use this optional first exercise to calm your mind and help you stay centered and balanced throughout your meditation session. I will discuss this more extensively in the next chapter.

Set Your Intention

Setting intentions is an essential part of daily life as well as spiritual practice. By setting an intention, you can develop increased awareness and mindfulness and better habits and behaviors.

In mindfulness techniques like meditation, an intention—which is comparable to a goal or objective—is often used. In the teachings of yoga, the term "intention" is related to the Sanskrit word "Sankalpa." San means "to become one with," while Kalpa means "subconscious mind." A Sankalpa/intention is, therefore, about getting in touch with your inner self and your greatest desire.

However, you don't have to be a meditation practitioner to set an intention. Anyone can perform a quick practice of setting intentions each day, week, or month. Setting an intent will help you become more motivated, disciplined, and productive because you'll have more focus and direction.

Why should you set intentions?

Setting intentions can help with a variety of aspects of spiritual and personal development.

We risk losing sight of our soul's ambitions and our life's purpose as a result of our hectic lives. We get caught up in the rat race when trying to make money or project a positive self-image to others. Setting goals and engaging in meditation help us disconnect from our daily lives and reconnect with our inner selves. From here, we can learn what we really want and how to get there.

Intentions can help you in gaining clarity as well as maintain focus and the proper course of action. They also offer accountability, which gives you more power to govern your life in the way you desire. Naturally, intention meditation helps you become more present in the moment by lowering stress and anxiety and boosting mindfulness.

How to set intentions for meditation

1. Self-reflect

If you're new to setting your intention for meditation, you might be unsure about how to start.

Sometimes our resolutions come to us immediately. For example, if we had a very stressful week, our intention might be to foster calm and peace.

However, finding the appropriate intention is not always easy. In these cases, I advise you to undertake some introspection. You might opt to write your responses down in a journal or simply consider them internally.

You should ask yourself the following three intention-setting questions before beginning your meditation session.

- What is most important to me right now?
- What am I able to let go of? Am I clinging to anything that is no longer helpful to me? Maybe a negative thought, regret, or resentment?
- How do I intend to show up today? What character traits and values are necessary for me to be the kind of person I aim to be?

2. Write it down

After mentally setting your intentions, put them in writing. Intentions are far more powerful when they are expressed in writing as opposed to just being thought about.

3. Examples of intentions

Since they are so individualized and can apply to any aspect of your life, there is no such thing as a wrong or right intention. However, the majority of people center their intention on their spiritual, physical, or mental well-being.

Intentions may be either short-term or long-term in nature. A short-term intention may be, for instance, how you want to feel today or this week. A long-term intention can be something you intend to implement to advance toward one of your most important goals or desires.

Just like affirmations, the most crucial aspect of setting an intention is to write it down in the present tense. Therefore, instead of saying you will do something, say it as though it is already true. Here are some intention examples:

- I show compassion and kindness to others.
- I favor harmony and love over hatred and hostility.
- I pursue a life of gratitude and appreciation.
- I take care of my spirit, mind, and body every day.
- I strive for harmony in every aspect of my life.
- I am patient and considerate toward others.
- I rest whenever I feel the need.
- I let go of every anxiety and fear that had been holding me back.

- I accept and welcome any change that comes my way.
- I place a high priority on my health.

For anything to become a habit, consistency is more crucial than frequency, such as how often you do it each week. Treat yourself with the respect you merit because this is a date with yourself. It's not necessary to do this every day, but do what seems comfortable unless or until you want to expand your practice.

4. Let it go

Surrendering is a crucial component in setting intentions. Remember that you only have a limited amount of power over your life. Therefore, all you can do is tell the universe what you want and then let it take care of the rest. Thus, let go of holding onto your intention too tightly and wishing and wanting it to come true. Instead, accept the freedom that comes from not being in charge of the outcome and trust that what is meant to be will come to pass.

Chapter Six

THE IMPORTANCE OF THE BREATH

"Train yourself in this way: from higher to higher; from strength to strength we will strive, and we will come to realize unsurpassed freedom." – Buddha

Anywhere you are, stop what you're doing right away and take a deep breath.

Most likely, you feel better now. It is well-recognized that taking a long, purifying breath will calm down our body's natural stress reactions and give us a sense of stability.

Breathwork is a new fad that is popular in the wellness world. A fast Google search will turn up articles and experts discussing its advantages, how it may be just as relaxing as meditation, and how it affects your mind, body, and spirit.

So, if breathwork sounds appealing to you, here is what you should know:

What is Breathwork?

The term "breathwork" refers to a variety of techniques that include using the breath deliberately. In essence, you can learn to control your breathing to harmonize your body and mind.

Today, we study the effects, but many cultures have long admired the power of breathing. Simple deep breathing exercises can be combined with more complex techniques. Breathwork is a simple, all-natural technique to improve your well-being.

How Does it Work?

When we breathe mindfully, the mind slows down and becomes more focused on the here and now. We feel relieved after that, which enables us to return to our daily activities with clarity and focus.

A brief rest can have a big impact on how relaxed and focused you are. Breathwork redefines the phrase "Take a Breather!"

What are Breathwork's Major Health Benefits?

The benefits of breathwork for our bodies are very well supported by science. The following are a few advantages of breathwork:

- Breathwork can help prevent an acute stress reaction and deflect the health issues brought on by persistent stress.
- Deep abdominal breathing lowers blood pressure by inducing the body's relaxation response.
- More sophisticated techniques, like Holotropic breathwork, have been shown to help the cathartic release of stress and trauma and improve addiction recovery.
- Breathwork improves bodily well-being, releases toxins, enhances immunity, and increases oxygen levels.
- It enhances digestion by increasing blood flow to the digestive tract.
- Improves happiness and self-esteem. Encourages mindfulness of the present, which results in a change of perspective.
- Enhances sleep. Soothes the nervous system and quiets the mind.
- Helps in managing discomfort. It allows your body to produce endorphins, which increase pleasure and reduce sensitivity.

Where did the Practice Originate?

Conscious breathing techniques to heal the body, mind, emotions, and spirit can be found throughout various cultures and historical eras.

Most significantly, breathwork has been continuously performed for healing and sustaining good health throughout China, India, Japan, and Tibet. Breathwork was documented as early as 2700 BCE in China and 3000 BCE in India. Since then, the procedures have been improved for contemporary use and are backed by empirical findings.

Types of Breathwork

You can try a lot of different breathwork exercises and approaches. Here are a few breath-control exercises that anyone can perform:

- Diaphragmatic breathing
- Box breathing
- Pursed lip breathing
- Alternate nostril breathing
- 4-7-8 breathing
- Breath focus technique
- Resonant breathing
- Equal breathing

After experimenting with the basic breathwork techniques, you might wish to learn more about an advanced breathwork technique to promote spiritual development and healing by attending a workshop or working with a trained expert. This comprises vivation, neurodynamic, somatic, transformational, holotropic, shamanic, rebirthing, pranayama, and SOMA breathwork.

This book will deal with the eight breathwork techniques for beginners and pranayama breathwork in the sections below.

Eight breathwork techniques for beginners

If you're ready to include breathwork in your wellness regimen, there are many quick breathwork exercises you can fit into your schedule to begin. Here are the top techniques you can start right away.

1. Diaphragmatic breathing

Diaphragmatic breathing is a type of breathwork that makes use of the stomach, abdomen, and diaphragm. It is sometimes known as belly breathing or abdominal breathing. It functions by making your diaphragm contract while you breathe, which allows your lungs to expand with more air. Here is how you do it:

- Lie down on a level surface or take a comfortable seat. To stay comfortable, you can either sit on a pillow or put them under your legs and head.
- Relax your shoulders.
- Put one hand on the top of your chest.
- The other hand should be placed on your tummy, between the diaphragm and ribs.

- Inhale slowly via your nose. As you push the air against your hand, concentrate on drawing it toward your stomach. Try to maintain a still chest.
- Exhale through your lips, tightening your abdominal muscles as you allow your stomach to drop and press downward. Keep making an effort to maintain chest stillness.
- Continue to breathe in and out as needed.

The science

The muscles surrounding our lungs often contract to provide room for them to expand with air as we breathe. The amount of air that enters your lungs at any given time is increased thanks to the help of diaphragmatic breathing during these contractions. We were all born to breathe properly; however, depending on our life experiences, this ability may change. We can change these ingrained habits by consciously exercising diaphragmatic breathing, which has several positive effects on our health. Diaphragmatic breathing has even been linked to improved focus and a reduction in negative emotions, according to a 2017 Frontiers study.

Benefits

- Helps in adjusting your breathing habits.
- Improves your ability to endure strenuous workouts.

- Reduces the possibility of straining or damaging your muscles.
- Reduces tension and fosters a sense of calm.
- Improves mental clarity.
- Increases the stability of your core muscles and diaphragm strength.
- Reduces oxygen demand by bringing down blood pressure and heart rate.
- Helps with asthma, COPD, PTSD, anxiety, depression, and other conditions.

2. Box breathing

Box breathing, often referred to as 4-4-4-4 breathing or square breathing, is a technique that helps in focusing on taking long, deep breaths. Many professionals and athletes use it to lower stress and improve performance. Here is how you do it:

- To get ready for this exercise, sit up straight and try to expel as much oxygen as you can by taking steady, deep breaths.
- Inhale slowly for four counts via your nose. Pay attention to the air entering your lungs.
- Hold your breath for four more counts.
- Exhale for a third count of four through your mouth. Pay close attention to how you feel as the air leaves your body.
- Hold your breath for another four counts.
- You can keep doing this as much as you like.

The science

Former Navy SEAL officer Mark Divine invented box breathing, which has been practiced since 1987. Due to its capacity to turn off a person's fight-or-flight mode, it is often used by people in high-stress states. This activity is regarded as a fantastic way to unwind because, when you pay close attention to your breathing, it diverts your attention from the stress around you. It is included as one of the numerous methods that have been shown to help relieve stress in the popular meditation software Headspace.

Benefits

- Makes it possible for you to relax and control your autonomic nervous system.
- It can help in controlling body temperature.
- It can help in reducing blood pressure.
- Lowers stress, boosts mood, and may even help treat depression, anxiety, panic disorder, and PTSD.
- When done before bed, it can help alleviate insomnia.
- It may be useful in managing discomfort.

3. Pursed lip breathing

Slowly inhaling and exhaling using pursed lips is known as pursed lip breathing. With the help of this technique, you can better regulate your breathing and increase the power of your breaths. Here is how you do it:

- Maintain a straight posture, whether sitting or lying down.
- Inhale through your nose for two counts. Do your best to feel the air entering your abdomen as well as your lungs.
- Squeeze your lips together and take four calm, deep breaths out. To complete this stage, you must always exhale twice as long as you inhale.
- Repeat as necessary.

The science

Through regular practice, pursed lip breathing has been shown to be beneficial for strengthening your lungs. This method is helpful for people with chronic lung illness and other ailments since it focuses on taking slower breaths and expelling stagnant air from your lungs. An investigation into the effects of pursed lip breathing in 2018 revealed benefits in COPD patients. It can serve as a supportive method during physically demanding activities like climbing stairs. It's important to keep in mind that this technique is most effective when practiced in a relaxed state.

Benefits

- Reduces breathlessness.
- Lessens the effort needed to breathe.
- Increases the amount of fresh air you are breathing in by releasing trapped carbon dioxide.
- Helps in the treatment of breathing disorders such as COPD, pulmonary fibrosis, and asthma.

4. Alternate nostril breathing

You can exercise breath control by breathing through your alternate nostrils. It is often performed during yoga or meditation, and pranayama breathwork can also incorporate it. Here is how you do it:

- Cross your legs as you sit down.
- Put your right hand up to your nose while placing your left hand on your left knee.
- Exhale, then use your right thumb to cover your right nose.
- Inhale from your left nostril, then close it with your fingers.
- Exhale from your right nostril after releasing your thumb from it.
- Inhale via your right nostril, then close it once again using your thumb.

- Put away your fingers from your left nostril, and exhale via this side. You've now finished a complete cycle.
- Repeat as many times as necessary, making sure to end each cycle.

The science

The theory behind alternate nostril breathing is that inhaling through your right nostril stimulates your left brain while breathing through your left nostril stimulates your right. The left part of our brains is associated with logic and language, while the right side is linked to creativity and emotions. By practicing alternate nostril breathing, you can activate both sides of your brain, promoting balance. Research suggests that this technique is effective in reducing stress levels.

Benefits

- Promotes relaxation.
- Lessens worry and tension.
- Improves heart rate and cardiovascular wellness.
- Improves respiratory endurance and lung capacity.
- Improves overall mental and physical health.

5. 4-7-8 Breathing

The 4-7-8 breathing method is based on pranayama breathwork, which will be covered in greater detail at the end of this section. It gives people control over their breathing and may even help them fall asleep. Here is how you do it:

- Make a whooshing sound as you part your lips and exhale through your mouth.
- Close your mouth and take four deep breaths via your nose.
- Hold your breath and count to seven.
- Repeat the whooshing sound while counting to eight while you breathe out with your mouth.
- Follow these instructions as much as needed.

The science

The 4-7-8 breathing technique is another breathing technique that encourages relaxation. It's been shown to be effective in modulating the fight-or-flight response and helping to manage feelings of stress and anxiety. It helps you achieve a state of serenity and makes it easier for you to fall asleep by forcing you to concentrate on your breathing rather than your anxieties.

Benefits

- Helps in mood regulation and reduces stress and anxiety.
- Helps in falling asleep and lessens tiredness.
- Lowers cravings.
- Decreases symptoms of asthma.
- Reduces high blood pressure.
- Reduces the symptoms of migraine.

6. Breath focus technique

Breath focus is commonly referred to as mindful breathing. It involves directing your attention toward specific thoughts, words, or phrases. Often, these thoughts or expressions can help create a sense of contentment, relaxation, or neutrality within. Here is how you do it:

- Find a relaxed position to sit or lie down.
- Pay close attention to your breathing. Try not to change your breathing pattern before using this technique.
- Alternate between deep breathing and regular breathing a few times, focusing on the differences between the two and the movements of your abdomen.
- Take a few shallow and deep breaths and notice how your shallow breaths differ from your deep breaths.
- Keep inhaling deeply for a few more minutes.

- Put a hand just below your belly button as you relax your tummy. As you continue to breathe, pay close attention to how it rises and falls.
- Exhale loudly each time you take a breath.
- As you keep inhaling deeply, start focusing on a calming thought, word, or phrase of your choice.
- Visualize your breath as a wave that calms and soothes your body. As you do this, you can mentally repeat the phrase "inhaling peace and calm."
- Visualize any negativity you're experiencing being swept away as you exhale. As you do this, you can mentally repeat the phrase, "exhaling tension and anxiety."
- The breath focus session is now over.

The science

The breath focus technique, like yoga, meditation, and various therapies, is known for its stress-reducing benefits. It's thought that paying attention to our breath can result in beneficial adjustments to our bodies and minds. Recent research has shown that focused breathing lights up specific areas of the brain related to emotions, attention, and body awareness. Based on the brain regions that lit up during concentrated breathing and rapid breathing, more investigations revealed that it could be used to reduce stress.

Benefits

- Decrease in stress and anxiety.
- Improvement in alertness and concentration.
- Strengthens the immunological system.
- Boosts vigor.

<u>7. Resonant breathing</u>

When we breathe at a rate of five breaths per minute, it is known as resonance or coherent breathing. It is a simple exercise that can be practiced anywhere with ease. Here is how you do it:

- Find a position that is relaxed for you.
- Breathe in for five counts, then exhale for five counts.
- Repeat these actions as necessary.

The science

Based on a 2017 study, resonance breathing has been found to have positive effects on heart rate and mood. When you practice resonance breathing, which involves breathing at a rate of five breaths per minute, it can increase your heart rate variability (HRV). This, in turn, helps reduce anxiety as your heart rate and neurological system are connected.

When paired with Iyengar yoga, this relieves stress and can help lessen depressive symptoms.

Benefits

- It relieves symptoms of depression, lowers stress and anxiety, and regulates the autonomic nervous system.
- Helps in blood pressure management.
- Alleviates asthma, COPD, fibromyalgia, and IBS symptoms.
- It may help in treating insomnia.

8. Equal breathing

Equal breathing, also known as sama vritti or circular breathing, is an activity that concentrates on making your inhales and exhales the same duration. This is done to help you feel balanced and calm by making your breathing smooth and steady. Here is how you do it:

- Find a comfortable seat.
- Inhale deeply through your nose and another one out.
- Count your inhales and exhales to ensure they are the same length. Pick a word or phrase to mentally repeat with each inhalation and exhalation if you find this uncomfortable.

- If it helps, you can also pause briefly between each inhalation and exhalation.
- You can carry out this activity for as long as you choose.

The science

Your parasympathetic nervous system is activated when you engage in equal breathing, gently ushering in a state of deep relaxation. A 2012 study highlighted its effectiveness in swiftly reducing stress and anxiety, offering a valuable tool for those seeking quick relief. In a manner reminiscent of counting sheep, equal breathing can be practiced as a soothing pre-sleep exercise. By directing your focus, it helps you find respite from worrisome thoughts, creating a serene space for your mind to unwind.

Benefits

- Relaxes your muscles.
- Helps you pay attention and concentrate better.
- Helps in mental peace.
- Enables you to breathe to your maximum potential.

Pranayama breathwork

Yoga breathing, also known as pranayama, encompasses a range of techniques aimed at cleansing the body and mind by eliminating impurities. When combined with yoga postures, it enables precise control of the breath with each movement. It is regarded as a spiritual technique for purifying the energy in your body and can be traced back to the earliest yogis of the Himalayas. By incorporating pranayama into your routine, you can experience a multitude of benefits, including stress and anxiety reduction, heightened focus, increased vitality, and a strengthened immune system.

There are many levels to this practice, but it is enough, while learning to meditate, to simply do the most basic type of pranayama breathing.

Below are a few basic types of pranayama breathing techniques:

- **Ujjayi Pranayama:** This breathing technique is also known as "ocean breath" because it emits a soothing sound resembling ocean waves. Before performing Ujjayi Pranayama, inhale deeply through your nose until your lungs are filled. Once you've done that, slowly exhale through your nose while tightening the back of your throat to produce a hissing sound. This technique is excellent for lowering anxiety and stress and enhancing focus.

- **Kapalbhati Pranayama:** This technique entails forceful nasal exhalations followed by passive inhalations. To perform Kapalbhati Pranayama, sit comfortably with your back straight, exhale deeply through your nostrils, and draw your belly toward your spine. After that, relax and allow your breath to come in naturally. This technique works wonders to cleanse the body and enhance digestion.

- **Bhramari Pranayama:** This breathing exercise involves humming while you breathe, which is claimed to have a relaxing impact on the mind. To perform Bhramari Pranayama, take a deep breath while sitting comfortably with your eyes closed. After that, carefully let out your breath while humming like a bee. Repeat several times. This technique is great for reducing stress and anxiety while improving mood.

These are just a few basic ones; there are many more pranayama breathing techniques to explore. By including pranayama in your daily practice, you can feel more relaxed, focused, and energized throughout the day, which can significantly positively affect your physical and mental health.

Pranayama is a practice of its own, more than 8,000 years old, and traditionally considered to be the foundation of yogic practices, whether yoga, meditation or just sitting with the breath for extended periods. It covers much more than I can fit into this book.

Chapter Seven

SIMPLE MEDITATION TECHNIQUES

"We are shaped by our thoughts; we become what we think. When the mind is pure, joy follows like a shadow that never leaves."–
Buddha

There are various types of meditation practices, each offering unique benefits. One of the best things about meditation is that it can be practiced at any time and in any place.

Most meditation methods are straightforward, ranging from simple breathing exercises to more intricate meditations.

Meditation is a deeply personal practice, as what brings solace to one person may be distracting to another. Guided meditations are a great alternative for those who find it hard to quiet their minds since they let them embark on amazing journeys.

In this chapter, we'll explore various meditation techniques, including common ones and mindfulness practices.

Engaging in a gentle meditation can transport you to different times and places, helping you release emotional baggage and let go of negative thoughts.

Meditation can help lift the layers of stress and anxiety that accumulate over time. By regularly practicing meditation, you can effectively manage stress, reduce tension, prevent depression, and even lower blood pressure.

I encourage you to experiment with these techniques to find the forms that best suit you - and there may be several, depending on time available, desire, and need.

Breath Awareness Meditation

While it's easy to find yourself in an endless cycle of battling your thoughts, there is a simple way to break free. The best part is, it only takes a few minutes out of your day. By tuning into your breath through breath awareness meditation, you can regain control of your life and feel intense feelings of peace, serenity, and relaxation throughout your mind and body.

The belief that you don't have enough time to integrate regular practice into your schedule is one of the most popular excuses for dodging meditation. However, you can begin experiencing the advantages of mindful breathing practice in just 5 minutes every day, and anyone can find an extra five minutes in their day, even if it means getting up a little earlier. Here is a short meditation on breath awareness that you may start incorporating into your everyday practice.

Step 1: Settle into a comfortable position

Choose a comfortable spot to sit on the floor or a chair with your feet firmly on the ground. Make sure your spine is long, and you are sitting up straight in either case. Your awareness becomes more present while you are sitting straight.

The goal is to bring about body stillness, leading to mental calmness. But if you're just starting, you could find that you need to adjust your posture when meditating. If you need to move, do so lightly and then focus again on your breathing.

Step 2: Close your eyes and observe the breath's natural rhythm

Close your eyes once you've settled into a comfortable position. Focus on the movement of the breath as it enters and exits the nostrils. Take note of the breath's natural rhythm as you inhale and exhale.

Are your breathing shallow or deep? Even or uneven?

Spend a few minutes in this position, simply watching the breath as it is. Don't attempt to manage or alter it. Simply let things happen spontaneously.

Step 3: Refocus your attention on your breath if it has wandered

If you're new to meditation, you'll probably find your mind wandering quite a bit. Try to notice any thoughts that come up without judging them.

Recognize the thought, then immediately return your focus to your breathing. The mind wandering will stop when your meditation practice becomes more regular.

Step 4: Examine the breath's movement through various bodily parts

If you're having trouble controlling your monkey mind, spend the rest of the session focusing on the breath coming in and out of your nostrils. Consider how it feels to accept your thoughts without passing judgment on them. Each time you become aware of a distraction, focus on your breathing.

You can try a body scan after you get the hang of returning to your breath. Observing how the breath fills the belly, chest, and neck is a terrific place to start. Keep an eye out for any physical sensations, stress, or resistance you may be retaining in a specific region as you observe.

Step 5: Refocus your attention on the room

After the five minutes are up, return your focus to your body. Slowly become aware of the space you're in and pay close attention to any sounds coming from outside. Take at least 30 seconds to rest here, but you can stay here as long as you need to acclimate. When you are ready, open your eyes and take a moment to recognize how your body and mind are feeling.

Since you're more awake and in touch with your senses at the end of a session, writing about your breath meditation in your notebook can also be a fantastic idea. Check out the emotion that arises for you and see how it changes over time.

Always keep in mind that meditation is a skill that requires consistency and effort to master. Respect where you are in your path, remain consistent and be kind to yourself. It's best to approach every session with a clear intention, avoiding the influence of others' experiences or even your own past encounters. Although every experience will be different, the key lies in dedicating time to alleviate your daily stress and nurture your overall well-being.

Body Scan Meditation

For many of us, stress manifests as mental and emotional symptoms and physical ones. Headaches, backaches, and heartburn are just some of the ailments stress can cause. Sometimes, we get so caught up in stress that we overlook the link between our mental and physical well-being. When that happens, a body scan meditation can provide great benefits. It allows us to connect with our bodies, check in with ourselves, and find effective relief from stress.

You can bring awareness to every region of your body by mentally scanning it from head to toe, imagining a laser copier scanning the length of your body to find any aches, pains, tension, or overall discomfort. Changing how we view pain, aches, and discomfort, staying present with them and breathing into them can help us feel better in our bodies and brains.

Body scanning is the best technique to detect alterations or interruptions in your body. Below are the steps for body scan meditation:

1. Take up your position. Locate a spot with little noise and distraction. Then, pick a comfortable posture for your body scan, whether you're lying or sitting down.

2. Draw a deep breath. Take several long breaths. Breathe gently and deeply from your diaphragm and out slowly and fully.

3. Pay attention. Be conscious of every physical interaction your body makes. Pay attention to how you physically feel as you sit or lie down. Take note of the surface's feel against your body.

4. Begin the scan. You have two options for starting the scan: start with your toes and work up or start at the top of your head and work your way down. No matter where you start, move slowly in one direction and note any odd, painful, or uncomfortable physical sensations.

5. Breath through it. Recognize any emotions or stress that arise as you scan each area of your body and pay attention to sensations. Take a moment to focus on the affected area and exhale deeply. Think about breathing the pain away or letting it go. If you feel any tension, let it out.

6. Check your entire body. A body scan is most effective when it covers your full body and assesses your feelings. Even if you are pain-free elsewhere in your body, it's crucial to fully assess your physical self before and after each meditation session. When you pay greater attention, you can find affected areas easier.

Anxiety-Relief Meditation

Interestingly, a key aspect of mindfulness practice is recognizing that staying still can sometimes make your thoughts race. The secret is to observe the mind without judgement. Start slowly with practice sessions that just last a few minutes. Gradually, you can extend your duration by establishing a more consistent, comfortable routine.

It's also crucial to meditate at a place where you won't be interrupted by people, animals, or phones or distracted by your environment. Take off your shoes, any bulky jewelry, and restrictive clothing. The idea is to meditate in a serene and cozy environment. After choosing a time and location, follow these four steps to lay the groundwork for your meditation practice.

Find a relaxed position

Many individuals choose to cross their legs and sit upright on the floor. However, you might find it more comfortable to lean back on a chair, sit up straight, or even lie down on your back. The goal is to find a comfortable position that allows you to stay focused without being too comfortable that you lose awareness or doze off. Remember, you can adjust your position at any time if you feel uncomfortable or have cramps.

Bring your attention to the present moment

Start turning your attention inward as soon as you're seated peacefully. Simply notice your breathing pattern without attempting to alter it; this will help you focus on the present moment. Start by closing your eyes. Bring the focus back to your breathing if your thoughts are straying. Once you have become aware of your breath's natural pattern, you can allow it to deepen to aid in relaxation.

Recognize your thoughts

At first, meditating can make you feel more anxious or judgmental of yourself. Am I doing it correctly? How should I proceed? Recognize that inner dialogue rather than trying to silence it and let it pass. As a result, you will remain silent while having uncomfortable thoughts. You will start to feel less worried and more at ease with yourself over time.

Complete your meditation

Open your eyes when you feel that your meditation is over. Come out of your meditation gradually and do some light stretches. Spend some time reflecting on your practice.

As mentioned earlier, during meditation, it might be challenging to keep track of time. If you're concerned that you'll exceed your allotted time, think about using a timer or alarm with a soft sound. Your focus will remain on your practice and not the timer.

Walking Meditation

Walking meditation is a form of focused awareness that combines the physical sensation of walking with a contemplative state. It allows you to connect your mind and body while you move and walk around, whether it's indoors or outdoors. With walking meditation, you have the freedom to determine the duration and pace of your session. During a walking meditation session, you focus on the feelings and movements of your body while walking or strolling for a certain period of time.

You can practice walking meditation within your home or outside in a park, wherever there is enough room for you to move about comfortably.

1. Pick a location. Practice mindful walking where you feel safe and have enough space to move about easily. While the environment need not be silent, it should be devoid of noisy distractions.

2. Begin to walk. Take 10 to 20 steps in a straight line while moving slower than usual. Put a foot in front of the other slowly and rhythmically, and take deliberate steps. At the end of those steps, turn around and proceed back in the same direction at a slow pace.

3. Be mindful. Take note of how your legs feel as you lift them off the ground and as they touch it. Keep track of any other feelings you get while walking. Your thoughts could begin to stray as you move along. To focus your mind, pay attention to the sounds and sensations of your breathing and steps. If there are sounds in the distance that you cannot tune out, simply notice them before turning your focus back to your breathing and walking. Spend a minimum of 10 to 15 minutes each day doing this.

4. Practice. Meditation while walking involves perseverance and practice. To benefit, try incorporating walking meditation as much as possible into your regular life.

Mindfulness Meditation

Mindfulness meditation is a mental exercise that teaches you to quiet your body and mind, let go of negativity, and slow down your racing thoughts. It minimizes impulsive and emotional reactions, lessens obsession with unpleasant emotions, enhances focus and memory, and boosts relationship satisfaction. It blends meditation with mindfulness, a mental state that entails being totally present in "the now" to accept and appreciate your thoughts, feelings, and sensations without judgment.

Although methods might differ, mindfulness meditation often entails deep breathing and awareness of one's body and mind. There is no need for preparation or props when practicing mindfulness meditation (unless you like using mantras, candles, or essential oils). All you need to begin is a relaxed spot to sit, three to five minutes of free time, and a mindset free of judgment.

Learning mindfulness meditation is simple enough to do on your own. Because it's a discipline, meditation is never flawless. As you are right now, you are ready to start!

Here are a few easy steps to get you going independently:

Be comfortable

Find a peaceful, cozy location. Sit on the floor or a chair with your head, neck, and back upright but not rigid. Wearing loose, comfortable dress will also help you concentrate.

However, a dress code is unnecessary as this activity can be performed anywhere for any length of time.

Consider using a timer

Even while it's not required, a timer (ideally with a soft, gentle alarm) can help you concentrate on your meditation and lose track of time, removing potential distractions.

It can also ensure you aren't meditating for an excessive amount of time because many people lose track of time while doing it. Don't forget to offer yourself time to become aware and slowly stand up after meditation.

While some people prefer longer sessions, even a short daily meditation session can have a positive impact. Start with a brief 5-minute meditation session and gradually extend them by 10 or 15 minutes until you feel comfortable meditating for 30 minutes.

Observe your breathing

Become attentive to the sensation of air entering and leaving your body while you breathe. As the air passes through and out of your nostrils, you'll feel your belly rise and fall. Pay attention to how the temperature changes between the inhaled and exhaled breath.

Take note of your thoughts

The objective is to become more at ease with being a "witness" to the thoughts rather than to stop thinking. Don't dismiss or suppress thoughts that come to mind. Instead, acknowledge them. Take note of them, stay composed, and use your breathing as a centering force. Like clouds passing by, watch your thoughts drift by as they fluctuate and change. The number of times you repeat this while meditating is up to you.

Take a break for yourself

If you notice that your thoughts are getting out of control—whether driven by worry, fear, anxiety, or hope—just observe where your thoughts have gone without passing judgment and return to breathing. If this happens, don't be too hard on yourself; mindfulness constantly brings your attention back to your breath and the present moment.

Install an App

Consider downloading an app (like Headspace or Calm) that offers free guided meditations and teaches you a range of methods to help you stay centered throughout the day if you're having problems practicing mindfulness meditation independently.

Progressive Relaxation Meditation

The Progressive Muscle Relaxation technique, which teaches you how to relax your muscles in two steps, is particularly helpful for people dealing with chronic pain. You start by intentionally tensing specific muscle groups, like your neck and shoulders. Then, you release the tension and focus on the sensations as your muscles gradually unwind. Thanks to this practice, you can relax when you're worried, which also helps you reduce overall tension and stress levels. It can also enhance your sleep and lessen physical issues like headaches and stomach aches.

People who struggle with anxiety are often so tense all day that they don't know what being relaxed feels like. By practicing the technique of tensing and releasing muscles, you can get better at telling the difference between the sensations of a muscle that is entirely relaxed and one that is tense. Then, at the first indication of the muscle tension that accompanies your sensations of fear, you can "cue" this calm state.

Getting ready

Find a spot to sit that is quiet and comfortable, then close your eyes and allow your body to relax. A reclining chair is a perfect option. You can lie down, but doing so will make it more likely that you'll fall asleep. Although unwinding before bed might enhance sleep, this practice aims to teach you how to unwind while awake. Don't forget to take off your shoes and dress in comfortable, loose-fitting clothes. Before you start, take five or more deep, steady breaths.

1. Tension

The first step is to gently tense the muscles in a specific area of your body. Whichever muscle group you are targeting, this process is essentially the same. Start by concentrating on the targeted muscle group, such as your left hand. Then, after taking a calm, deep breath, squeeze your muscles for roughly 5 seconds. Notice how tight your muscles are; they might even feel uncomfortable or start to shake in this situation.

Try to only contract the muscles you are targeting because it is easy to unintentionally tense other muscles (such as the shoulder or arm). With practice, separating muscle groups becomes easier.

Be careful! Avoid injuring yourself by not tensing your muscles too hard. You shouldn't experience sharp shooting pain when performing this exercise. Aim to create a gentle and mild tension in your muscles. Consult your doctor first if you have trouble with torn muscles, fractured bones, or other health conditions that might stop you from engaging in physical activity.

2. Relaxing the stiff muscles

Now it is time to relax the stiff muscles. Give them permission to release their tension after about 5 seconds. Exhale as you complete this action. As the tension releases, you should feel the muscles becoming limp and relaxed. Take a moment to consciously observe the difference between the sensations of tension and relaxation. The focus of the entire exercise should be on this.

It may take some practice to become aware of the difference between tension and relaxation in the body. Awareness of your body may initially feel strange, but it can eventually be satisfying.

After around 15 seconds, relax before moving on to the next muscle group. Repeat the tension-release exercises. Take some time to savor the profound state of relaxation once all the muscle groups have been worked on.

Spiritual Meditation

Spiritual meditation allows you to delve into the essence of who you are. Without all of the self-perceptions you had up until that moment, you are your genuine self. You benefit from the process by experiencing joy and peace. Your entire self begins to warm up with a sense of brightness and love.

Realizing the eternal truth through spiritual meditation helps you let go of everything that has happened and will happen in the future. You want to be and are at peace in the present. The need to see and think beyond your confusing world drives the urge for spiritual meditation. Now, let's learn how to do it.

1. Choose a relaxed position

The most crucial step is to find a location and position you will feel comfortable in before you start the exercise. This entails removing yourself as much as you can from city noises and surrounding yourself with vegetation and the tranquil chirping of birds. You can fall asleep very quickly during spiritual meditation. You must be especially careful when choosing the position you want to meditate in to avoid that. Select a comfortable posture, but avoid one that is very soothing and causes you to nod off easily. Additionally, you can stand up with your back against a wall or sit on a chair with a straight back. Whatever works. Now, gently close your eyes.

2. Experience the process

What do you typically do when you have a task to complete? You prepare, mentally follow the steps, and consciously follow the pattern. We typically complete tasks in this manner. We carefully prepare for them and carry them out. This, however, is not the best method to approach meditation. You will need to let it go at this point. Relax and allow it to take its course organically and naturally. You ought to mentally stand back and watch while the process unfolds naturally. Don't worry about doing things correctly or worrying about the result. Allow it to flow naturally.

3. Acknowledge the thoughts

The world in which we live is information-based. You are constantly fed fresh information through social media, breaking news, and live updates. Your mind is constantly active due to new information and your brain's response. As long as you are awake, it is a never-ending game, and even when you are asleep, it might be difficult to quiet your racing thoughts.

Every thought causes a reaction, and you inevitably become impacted by it. You will be distracted by thoughts even as you sit in meditation. However, the difficulty is being silent and letting them influence you. Allow the thoughts to flow as they typically do, but resist the impulse to respond to them. Allow them to vanish so you can return to your meditation.

4. Say a prayer or affirmation

Choose a prayer or affirmation in your mind as you sit there, stopping your thoughts from undermining your calm composure. Prayer need not have any religious overtones. Any phrase with positive connotations for you or that you find appealing is acceptable. It might be a word or a sentence. If you enjoy nature, it might be something related to wildlife or something that makes you happy. It may even be a mantra.

Now, maintain a loose, relaxed body. Breathe normally and gradually. Watch your breath as it comes and goes. Your process is interrupted by thoughts, but you know how to deal with them. Every time your thoughts wander, return to your physical being and breathing. Then, when you exhale, consider the prayer or affirmation you selected.

Every time you exhale, repeat it to yourself in your brain. Use the statement as a tool to return your focus to noticing your breath.

5. Examine yourself

Focus on your body and your awareness and presence in the space. Pay attention to your surroundings. Consider how your body is feeling. Pay close attention to your breathing and thoughts. Embrace a state of complete calm and relaxation. Slowly open your eyes and remain seated for some minutes. Let meditation's benefits settle in. Feel it, and take pleasure in how light your body feels. Reflect on the entire process and your approach. Take note of how calmer you are than before the meditation. Recognize that it was natural for you to react the way you did.

Finally, leave the meditation state, stretch briefly, and resume your normal activities.

Guided Meditation

This style of guided meditation is all about noticing or recognizing what is happening and letting whatever is experienced be without any judgment, resistance, or grasping. You are developing the ability to pay close attention to how your body genuinely feels while observing the thoughts that arise, all without feeling the need to "problem-solve" or make any changes. You learn more about yourself by keeping an open mind, including your experiences, feelings (good, bad and neutral), thoughts, and emotions.

Remember that the practices you engage in during meditation are supposed to be applied to the rest of your life. Most of the 16 hours of waking day you're not alone in meditation are while you're out and about, interacting with others and life's happenings. The instructions you'll learn during guided meditation are all intended to make it easier to apply the practice, attention, and understanding of your regular thoughts and habits to the rest of your life, where they matter.

1. First, make an intention.

Your intentions will determine what is feasible during your guided meditation and the takeaways and applications you'll get from it. According to a Zen meditation precept, "The most significant thing is remembering the most significant thing." In other words, establishing an intention before you meditate might help you remember why you do it in the first place and serve as your "anchor" while practicing. Perhaps you meditate to improve your relationships, be more productive at work, or be compassionate to your spouse, partner or loved ones. These are all admirable goals to return to when your mind wanders.

2. Give your body some time to unwind

Try to unwind your body when you begin meditation and gradually practice letting go. Pay attention to your jaw, eyebrows and the area surrounding your eyes, forehead, chest, belly, and neck, where you probably carry some tension. With each exhale, deliberately let go a little more (almost like when you fall asleep) while softening these areas. You can now pay attention to the ins and outs of your breathing as a skill meant to quiet down the mind. You can also perform a body scan meditation to relax by concentrating on your scalp and gradually descending to your toes while releasing each place.

3. Keep an eye on your senses

Start focusing more on specific sensations (such as hearing, how the chair or floor feels beneath you, the temperature, and any scents) and begin to sense your body. By concentrating on your physical sensations, you can ground yourself and calm your racing thoughts. What specifically are you sensing? Vibrations? Pulsing? Colors? Lightness? Heaviness? Whatever you discover while examining your feelings, keep in mind that you don't have to strive to change them or drive them away; you can simply accept them as they are. If it helps you maintain attention, use your breath as a consistent backdrop or anchor as you continue to explore how it feels in your body. This is the technique of learning to accept whatever is happening without resistance, and it may be applied outside of the context of meditation.

4. Investigate your feelings

You might want to do more investigating at this point. Check to see if anything bothers you, makes you uncomfortable or difficult, or brings any particularly bad memories to mind. If your thoughts stray, keep track of where they are. This can be done by telling yourself that you are "planning" or "remembering," for instance.

5. Continue returning to the body

Recognize the thoughts that arise and acknowledge them for what they are: mere thoughts that have no bearing on reality or even the truth. Always remember that just because you have an opinion or judgment about something doesn't mean it is true. Avoid adding to the thoughts with additional emotions or allowing yourself to veer off into a tangent about the past or future as much as possible. As you strive to disengage from the thoughts entering your head, keep returning to the sensations of your body and breath. Remember that while you could hear a voice telling you what you should be thinking about, this is just your mind doing what it does best—wandering aimlessly! The basic idea is that you don't have to act on every thought you have or consider it true; instead, you can respond but not react to what is happening in your environment.

The benefits of meditation for the body and mind have been known for ages, and now research can support these claims. A wonderful place to start is with guided meditation. Yes, effort and patience are required, but trust me, it will be well worth it.

The advantages of guided meditation extend beyond just reducing stress. The risk of depression, chronic pain, obesity, binge eating, emotional eating, poor sleep, chronic illness recovery, and other conditions have all been decreased by meditation. So, don't wait; start meditating right now.

Mantra Meditation

Chanting or employing mantras during meditation has a special calming effect. Research has shown that mantra meditation can help you quiet your mind's racing thoughts and relax your body. Additionally, it can lessen distractions, lengthen concentration spans, and enhance your mood and mental state. Also, practicing it is fairly easy.

Here, I outline the procedures for performing a mantra meditation. You should engage in this meditation every day for anywhere between 5 and 20 minutes, or even longer if you feel the need or want. Steps 1 and 2 should be completed in one to two minutes, Step 3 in three to five minutes, and Step 4 in five to fifteen minutes.

Step 1

Choose a favorite word, phrase, affirmation, prayer, or passage from poetry to begin meditation. A mantra should ideally only have a few syllables or words so you can repeat it without getting lost in a lengthy phrase. Pick an uplifting word that touches your heart and encourages you. Avoid using terms that make you think or make you anxious.

Step 2

Take a seat comfortably, either in a chair or on the floor. Use a cushion or a blanket to support your posture. Find a comfortable position that aligns with the spine's natural curvature so you can stay there for a while. Take a few calm, deep breaths while closing your eyes, or spend some time practicing breathing techniques before completely relaxing your breath.

Step 3

Repeat your mantra slowly and steadily, focusing on its sound as intently as you can. It should be repeated in time with your breathing's natural rhythm. Either divide the mantra in half and repeat it twice—once when you inhale and once when you exhale—or repeat it both times.

Step 4

Repeat the mantra silently by only moving your lips after around 10 repetitions (this helps you maintain a consistent tempo). After another 10 repetitions, repeat the phrase silently in your head without moving your lips.

Step 5

Simply repeat the mantra as thoughts come to mind, understanding that this is a normal part of the process. Bring your focus back repeatedly, being as present with the internal sound as possible.

Step 6

Continue for the duration of your dedicated hour of meditation. Take a few deep breaths to exit the meditation, then sit quietly to evaluate your feelings. You might sense peace and balance. Or, you can experience uncomfortable flooding from repressed memories and sensations.

Regardless of how you feel right now, rest assured that daily practice has many advantages, including the ability to fully experience the here and now and avoid defaulting to automatic responses.

'Do Nothing' Meditation

While "do nothing meditation" may imply that you simply sit and...do nothing, it's not simple. But the good news is that it isn't much harder than that, either. This is the method to use if you're looking for a means to unwind.

This type of meditation is derived from shikantaza, which can be loosely translated as "just sitting." And that's exactly what you'll do when you start practicing this type of meditation. You'll simply sit and engage in your practice. There are no exercises for deep breathing, walking, or difficult guided instructions to follow.

You might be ready to embark on this soothing exercise. But it's important to keep in mind that this type of meditation can be quite challenging. It's amazing that you can do things independently without assistance, but doing nothing is much tougher than it may seem. Because of this, many experts believe this is one of the more complex forms of meditation.

Here's how to begin this kind of meditation if you're ready to give "doing nothing" a try.

Find a comfortable position. When practicing do nothing meditation, there is no wrong way to sit or lie down. Remember that this is not a nap if you decide to lie down while practicing meditation. Most experts advise finding a comfortable position while seated on a cushion or meditation stool.

Don't concentrate on any one thing in particular. Don't concentrate on anything in front of you or think about anything in particular. Instead of using gongs, noise signals, or other instructions to help you focus, concentrate on simply being.

Allow whatever happens to just... happen. The idea is to just sit there and watch the world go by.

If you catch yourself acting in any way, stop. Stop doing or concentrating on anything when you catch yourself doing it on purpose. If you are doing something that you have the power to stop doing, do so voluntarily. This is much more difficult than it first appears, but if you can do one thing intentionally, you can stop the same thing intentionally.

Repeat this process for a total of 10-15 minutes. The objective is to set aside enough time to focus solely on doing nothing, though you can extend your meditation practice if you'd like.

There is no wrong way to do this form of meditation unless you find yourself actively doing anything or thinking about something while you sit, which is one of the beautiful things about this meditation. Remember that if you do something purposefully, you are not engaging in do-nothing meditation.

Nature-Inspired Meditation

These meditations take place outside in the open air. They help bring forth nature's basic intelligence in our physiology and awareness. The sight of a flower, the sound of birds, and the sensation of the breeze all resonate with our essence. These experiences arouse something within us and help our lives become more organic. Nature enthusiasts found this trick without ever learning meditation!

During nature meditations, you'll concentrate on the sensory perceptions of nature, including sight, sound, touch, smell, and sometimes even taste. As with every meditation, gently bring the mind back to the meditation whenever it strays. This meditation can be practiced in a variety of ways. Try different ways to see what suits you the best.

Eyes closed

Choose a sitting or laying position that feels comfortable. Start by taking some slow, deep breaths from the belly to help you relax and bring your awareness to the sensations of the present moment. Now close your eyes and pay attention to what is happening when they are closed. Notice the sensations in your body and observe the activity of your mind and emotions. Simply be with what is without attempting to change or resist anything. Spend about a minute doing this.

Now bring your focus to all you can perceive in your immediate environment. Feel the air's temperature, the breeze, and the sun's rays on your skin. Take note of the nearby sounds, such as birds, bees, crickets, and running water. Pay attention to nature's symphony. Continue to be aware of these sensations and sounds for the remainder of the meditation. When your thoughts stray, gently draw them back to your time in nature.

You can watch where your attention naturally falls during meditation or actively scan for various experiences. You can also concentrate on a single experience and pay closer attention to it. If it is a bird's song, pay attention to the sound's quality as if you were delving deeper into it. It could appear to have a shape or a certain texture. Simply take note of the sound's quality rather than trying to analyze and categorize it.

Once more, as you become aware that your thoughts have taken over your mind, simply return it to the sights, sounds, and feelings of being in nature. There will occasionally be awareness of both thoughts and environmental experiences. It's alright. Just easily lean towards nature's experience.

Listening

Start as instructed in the Nature-inspired Meditation, focusing solely on sound. Allow your consciousness to be with all the sounds around you as you pay close attention to each one. You might also concentrate on a certain sound like water flowing. When your mind wanders, keep bringing it back to that particular sound.

Eyes open

You can practice this meditation while sitting, standing, or moving around. Spending time in nature can be a meditation if we focus entirely on everything around us, including the ground, trees, flowers, animals, fresh air, and the breeze.

Allowing yourself to take in the sights, sounds, and smells can help fully immerse yourself in the event. Be aware of your mind's propensity to categorize and judge everything: "Oh, look at that lovely bird. Which kind is it? Does it stay here all winter, or does it leave?" Let these kinds of thoughts go when they happen. Simply pay attention to the sounds, colors, shapes, movements of the bird and anything else you notice. Let it be a meaningless experience that is unrelated to any previous experiences.

As if you've never encountered anything similar, approach every event with an open awareness. Always bring the mind back to the nature experience when it starts to stray or become preoccupied with thoughts.

There is a meditation technique for everyone, whether the goal is to gain spiritual enlightenment or reduce stress. Try new things, and don't be scared to venture outside your comfort zone. Finding the right one often involves some trial and error.

It's not intended for meditation to be forced. When we push it, it turns into a task. The slow, consistent practice gradually develops into something sustaining, encouraging, and delightful.

Allow yourself to consider all the options. There are many different types of meditation; if one isn't effective or comfortable, try another.

Chapter Eight

RESOLVING PITFALLS WHEN MEDITATING

"What we are today comes from our thoughts of yesterday, and present thoughts build our life of tomorrow: our life is the creation of our mind"–
Buddha

If we're having trouble meditating, it's likely because we're trying too hard to regulate our thoughts and practice. Even though we wish it were, meditation isn't mind control, sorcery, or a superpower. It's a technique that teaches us to accept our thoughts exactly as they are. We don't aim to feel a specific way, change our thoughts, condemn them, or attempt to stop thinking completely while we meditate. Even when one is meditating, thoughts will still enter the mind.

Let's picture our brain as a freeway and our thoughts as vehicles traveling down it. Try it now: Is the road clear? Is there traffic today? Our minds may be spinning with thoughts. Do you think a large truck honks its horn to draw our attention to something? Or are there roadblocks in every lane?

There is no right or wrong response. It feels like we are keeping track of a fresh traffic report every time we check in with our minds. We have no control over how many cars are on the road or how long the commute takes, just like real-world traffic. Even though we may not enjoy the traffic speed or the road conditions, we manage to deal with it (preferably without erupting in road rage) and finally arrive at our destination.

While daily meditation helps us to develop the conditions necessary to experience the peace and tranquility of driving down a wide-open road, it's also true that we might not feel at ease and comfortable right away. So, to make meditation easier, we might lower our expectations and consider these advantages as a byproduct of meditation rather than the intended outcome. Being present and letting go of thoughts and feelings as they arise are the only objectives of meditation. Then, when we become sidetracked, we return to our breath and remember that, despite our challenges, we are doing just fine.

How Do I Overcome Common Meditation Problems?

Like thoughts, we can usually overcome obstacles in meditation if we can confront them with compassion and let them go rather than fight them. You'll discover how to achieve that with this guide on resolving 17 of the most prevalent meditation issues. Let's make meditation easy on ourselves.

1. What should I do if I don't have time to meditate?

We only need a short period to meditate. Even a 1-minute breathing practice can help us if we've never meditated. Or we might begin with a 3- or 5-minute guided meditation and progressively increase the length. However, if we're stressed and overwhelmed, finding and protecting the time for a quick meditation can be difficult. The fix is to include meditation in a regimen that already exists. By linking it to something familiar, our minds are tricked into becoming less resistant to it. Every time we turn off our alarm in the morning, get out of the shower, brush our teeth, brew a cup of coffee, or tuck ourselves into bed—whatever works—try meditating.

2. What if I'm meditating the wrong way?

There is no good or bad way to meditate, in actuality. When beginning something new, thoughts like "Am I doing this right?" are common. The mind's default action is to create opposition, whether it be doubt about our practice or a justification for not meditating. It only becomes an issue when we give in to that inner voice and believe what it says. We can let it go and shift our attention back to our breathing after recognizing it for what it is—just another thought. It's okay to continue doing this during the entire meditation. Every day, and perhaps every practice, will feel different as you train your mind to let go.

3. How do I keep up my regular meditation practice?

We simply don't want to meditate sometimes! But when we are certain of why we are doing it, our purpose of sitting with the mind becomes easier without understanding our "why," we often give up once the first thrill of trying something new wears off. Think for a moment about why you wish to practice everyday meditation. Are you trying to be less receptive to that one thing your partner does? Be less enticed by social media so that you can spend more time with the people you care about? Better balance between work and life? Catch your breath after diaper duty? Reduced level of concern about the future? Establish a self-care schedule? It's ok if this drive evolves with time. But the easier it is to apply, the clearer it will be.

4. Why am I unable to focus during meditation?

One of the major misconceptions about meditation is the idea that we must "clear" or "empty" the mind to succeed; however, this is not true. The truth is that thinking never stops. And we often do it: We lose ourselves in contemplation for over half of our waking hours. Only when we minimize outside distractions, such as meditating, does it become clear to us.During meditation, our only duty is to acknowledge wandering thoughts and then let them go. We can try identifying them to make this process easier. Next time your thoughts start to stray, for instance, simply say, "Thinking," and then slowly bring your attention back to your breathing. We can do the same with feelings.

5. Why am I finding meditation to be so boring?

Even if we are certain about our "why," boredom is unavoidable; even for seasoned meditators, all of us are accustomed to staying active, juggling multiple tasks, and looking ahead. We pause and concentrate on a few repetitive actions during meditation, such as breathing in and out and allowing our thoughts to come and go numerous times. This is all much less mentally stimulating. When there is undoubtedly something more entertaining or productive to do, we can ask, "What's the point?" However, let's remember that this thought is just one among many. If we succumb to it and move quickly to something more exciting, we never allow our minds to relax and teach them to ignore peaceful times. Stick with it, examine it, and see where it leads us instead of fighting boredom. We might observe that "boredom" is only a symptom of our everyday feelings of fatigue, burnout, or dissatisfaction.

6. Why do I become restless while meditating?

While meditating, if we find ourselves fidgeting or our minds racing to the past or future, it's a sign that we're having trouble attaining stillness. It's completely normal and understandable. However, because many of us think being restless is "bad," we try to stop by willpower, which only leads to further agitation and anxiety. Try to let it go, just like any other thought, without resisting, and shift your attention back to your breathing. Instead of getting caught up in thoughts like "I'm restless," we can find greater ease by simply focusing on the rhythm of our breath. To calm the mind before meditation, try slowing down in the minutes leading up to it if you're still having problems remaining still or controlling rushing thoughts. The mind and body need time to calm down after a long day of activity; slamming on the metaphorical breaks won't make them suddenly still.

7. Can I ever become proficient at meditation?

If we were learning to bake, we wouldn't try to make a wedding cake after our first few attempts. The same goes for learning to meditate. Despite this, even novices and experienced professionals encounter mental distractions. The difference is that they have mastered accepting their thoughts without condemning them. Let's practice self-compassion the next time we are trying to criticize or talk negatively to ourselves while meditating. Teaching the mind to let go is continual, and every day is different. That is why meditation is called "practice," after all.

8. What causes my impatience while meditating?

During meditation, impatience can manifest in many different ways. Perhaps we want to get started right away in a guided meditation because we have somewhere to be, or we may feel that our meditation practice isn't progressing quickly enough. Whatever the impatience, we may let it go because it is only a thought. Instead of telling ourselves that we need to be more patient, we might work on letting go of our expectations of how life ought to be. The more often we do this, the more at ease we can become with where we are in both our daily lives and practice. We might even observe that we are inherently more patient and compassionate toward others' lack of patience.

9. How can I remain at ease while meditating?

We won't likely feel at ease during our practice if we don't feel at ease before we begin to meditate. Select a location where you can sit in an alert position for a while. Try sitting at the front of the chair to maintain a straight back and stretch the spine. If it isn't sufficient to support, you can shift to a couch, lie down if you're tired, or add a cushion to the chair. Still, feeling restless when meditating? This is normal. As we slow down, we tend to become more conscious of our bodily experiences. Decide to stay with the session until the end if there is no severe pain. Drive your attention back to your breath (over and again, if required) and acknowledge the need to move or stand up without criticizing or attempting to change it.

10. How do I handle distractions when meditating?

We must stop meditation if a child climbs on us, a dog licks our face, or the doorbell rings. And it's very acceptable to do that. We can resume where we left off or start anew after dealing with that interruption. Other distractions, such as a ringing phone, music played by a neighbor or even sirens, are not an excuse to stop or give up. We can't make them go away, no matter how much we want them to. Therefore, the greatest action is to release our resistance and return to our breath. We can even say "welcome" to the crashing construction, the clanging radiator, or other noisy interruptions to relieve our minds. It would be comforting to remember that when we become aware of being distracted, we are fully aware of our surroundings. We become more conscious as we focus on our thoughts, feelings, emotions, and distractions.

11. Why do I keep falling asleep in the middle of meditation?

Dozing off during meditation is normal, so there's no need to feel frustrated about it. We might need to explore a little to balance concentration and relaxation. Begin by avoiding lying down to meditate or by trying to meditate elsewhere. You can splash cold water on your face beforehand, open a window for fresh air, or even meditate outside while running

or strolling if meditation still makes you want to hit
the snooze button.

12. What should I do if I have a bothersome itch when meditating?

Because we see that uncomfortable itch as something
unpleasant or inconvenient that we want to
eliminate, we want to scratch it out of habit. While
you're meditating, try not to. Why? The mind is being
trained to be less reactive and more tolerant of your
body and mind as they are. You can develop
mindfulness and responsiveness that will benefit
your daily life if you learn to sit with the sensation
and become intrigued about how it shifts and moves.
Give it a beat if you happen to be itchy. You can
acknowledge, "Ah, I have an itch," and shift your
attention back to the breath. If you sit with it long
enough, the feeling might go away. Have a scratch if
it keeps happening. Just be mindful that it becomes
harder for the mind to calm down as the body moves.

13. How should I handle stress or anxiety when meditating?

When we meditate, stress or anxious thoughts may
feel even stronger since we are sitting still, perhaps
for the first time all day or all week. That is typical.
Most of us try to ignore our anxious thoughts
because we don't like these sentiments. However, it
doesn't negate their existence and doesn't lessen our

anxiety. It usually has the opposite effect—we become mired in a cycle of fearful thoughts. Focus on any physical anxiety symptoms, such as stomach butterflies, to stop it. We can avoid worrying more readily when leaving the mind and entering the body.

14. How can I manage my anger or frustration while meditating?

No aspect of our day, including our meditation, must be derailed by intense emotions. It may seem that way because we tend to repress things, yet the more we do so, the more forcefully they reappear. Take them on head-on rather than try to escape them. To achieve this, consider shifting your attention away from your inner conversation, such as "I'm so angry!" and onto the bodily sensations it is causing, just like you did with the itch. Do you feel warm? Do you have your jaw or fists clenched? Are you frowning? When we practice mindfulness in the heat of the moment, we can deal with our anger rather than adding gasoline to the fire. We can apply a variety of anger-reducing meditation practices if we find that we continue to be easily agitated.

15. How should I handle sadness when meditating?

Like worry, sadness is normal; it's neither a sin nor a sign of frailty. While meditating, it's normal to feel a lump in the throat or a few tears, which is nothing to be afraid of, ashamed of, or consider inconvenient. During meditation, you shouldn't suppress your emotions if you feel like crying. Flow with it. Take a break from meditation, if necessary, to let your feelings have their say. This kind of acknowledgment of something uncomfortable may help relieve you of it.

16. How can I avoid thinking about meditation while doing it?

We're used to pushing ourselves to work harder and do things correctly in our daily lives, so it's understandable that we would try to overcomplicate meditation as well. There is no good or bad way to meditate, though. By overanalyzing our meditation, we risk making it more difficult than it should be. Instead, keep your attention on your breathing while allowing your ideas to come and go. Meditation-related thinking is just like any other thought. So, classify them as "thinking," just like we do with others, and allow them to drift off.

17. How can I manage discomfort when meditating?

Feeling discomfort during meditation, such as physical tightness, is fairly usual. To welcome discomfort seems a little backward. But recognizing it and becoming friends with it can help you cope with aches and pains. Try focusing more on how you respond to the soreness after you become aware of it than on the actual discomfort. In this manner, you can look into what's bothering you. Is it a specific location or a broad area? Is there a specific shape to it? Is the discomfort sharp or lingering? Does the pain feel static, or does it move around? It can be intriguing to explore the pain rather than being critical or judgmental if the pain begins and ends with one's practice. This enables us to change how we feel pain to something more controllable. It can be wise to speak with a healthcare provider if the pain begins with your practice but doesn't go away when you open your eyes.

Meditation has many advantages, but it's not always easy to begin. When you first begin meditating, you could run into certain challenges. However, don't allow that to prevent you from enjoying the benefits of this routine. Use the tips in this chapter to overcome these difficulties and take advantage of meditation.

Chapter Nine

HEALTH BENEFITS OF MEDITATION AND MINDFULNESS

"If your sense-organs are calm, so will the acts of the body become calm, calm the acts of speech, calm the acts of the mind."–
Buddha

Meditation is rather wonderful. Its benefits have been extensively researched and proven. While it's commonly known for lowering stress and anxiety, studies suggest that it can also enhance mood, support sound sleep habits, and sharpen cognitive abilities.

When you engage in meditation, you're training your mind to stay focused and let go of distractions. As more people discover its many physiological benefits, meditation is quickly gaining recognition and popularity.

It allows us to become more mindful of our surroundings and selves. Many consider it a means of lowering stress and improving focus.

On top of all that, meditation is also a great tool for developing positive qualities and emotions. It can help you have a more positive outlook on life, improve self-control, enhance your sleep quality, and even increase your ability to handle pain.

In this chapter, I'll show you the 10 physiological benefits of meditation.

Stress Management

Studies published in the Clinical Psychology Review have shown that mindfulness-based practices, such as meditation, have positive effects on mental well-being, especially when it comes to managing stress. When facing challenging or stressful situations, our bodies release cortisol, a hormone responsible for regulating our stress response and fight-or-flight response, among other functions. Chronic stress can result in persistently high levels of cortisol, harming your immune, digestive, and cardiovascular systems and overall health. Fortunately, meditation can help alleviate the impact of chronic stress on the body by concentrating on calming the mind and controlling emotions.

Anxiety Management

Controlled breathing and slowing down racing thoughts through meditation can help deal with the effects of anxiety, such as overpowering sensations of fear, concern, and tension. This helps to relax the nervous system. When anxiety takes hold, it may manifest in physical ways like sweating, feeling lightheaded, or having a fast heartbeat. These sensations arise when our minds become consumed with constant thoughts about the past or future. A study published in General Hospital Psychiatry discovered that people with anxiety who regularly practiced meditation for three years saw positive, long-term effects on their mental well-being.

Depression Control

Meditation has a way of controlling depression by helping people tune in and take control of their emotions. This was seen during a study at a three-month meditation retreat where participants saw a significant decrease in depressive symptoms and enhanced resilience to stress and overall well-being.

Reduced Blood Pressure

Around one billion individuals are believed to be affected by hypertension, also known as high blood pressure. In the United States alone, nearly half the population deals with this issue. But the good news is, meditation has been seen to bring these numbers down, particularly when combined with healthy lifestyle practices, including a balanced diet and exercise. Although evidence supports the use of meditation for decreasing blood pressure, we still need more research to figure out exactly how different types of meditation can have an impact.

Enhances Immune System Health

Meditation has also been discovered to be an effective behavioral therapy for several illnesses linked to a compromised immune system. Regularly practicing meditation can work wonders for our body's stress response, which means less inflammation and a lower chance of dealing with things like chronic pain, weariness, and heart disease.

Improves Memory

Did you know that meditation does more than just help with stress and anxiety? It can also change how your brain is wired. Studies have shown that meditation increases the amount of gray matter your brain can produce. The hippocampus, the brain area connected to memory, is protected by gray matter and is essential for good brain cognition. Basic human functions, such as our capacity to control our emotions and movements, also depend on it. The same study discovered that practicing meditation 30 minutes a day for eight weeks can boost your body's production of gray matter.

Regulates Mood

When practiced regularly, meditation can change how you emotionally respond to situations. Mindfulness and controlled breathing are two common meditation techniques that help people act less impulsively. This implies that regular meditation practitioners can develop the ability to better control their mood rather than reacting from a heightened emotional state like anger or fear.

Heightens Self-Awareness

By forming the practice of concentrating on the present moment, meditation helps you become more aware of your thoughts as they arise. According to research, meditation can improve impulse control, foster a healthier relationship with oneself and others, and promote self-awareness.

Helps with the Management of Addiction

Individuals who struggle with substance use disorders can discover solace through the calming and grounding effects of meditation. By cultivating a sense of inner tranquility and fostering mindfulness in the present moment, meditation offers a valuable tool for managing triggers and reducing the likelihood of relapse to cope with other mental health issues like stress or anxiety.

Improves Sleep

According to research, meditation can enhance a person's sleep capacity and quality. Many of us struggle to fall asleep because our minds are occupied with thoughts of the day or what lies ahead. While more research is required to validate how meditation improves sleep, it has shown promising results in alleviating insomnia and related issues such as daytime fatigue.

Everyone can benefit from meditation in terms of mental and emotional well-being. With no memberships or specialized equipment required, you can do it anywhere.

As an alternative, support groups and meditation classes are readily accessible. There are many styles, each with unique advantages and capabilities.

Even if you have less than 10 minutes to meditate each day, it's a fantastic idea to experiment with a style that aligns with your goals.

Chapter Ten

YOUR 10-STEP PLAN FOR REGULAR MEDITATION

Meditation is effective for fostering inner calm, lowering stress levels, and improving general well-being. But for many people, starting a regular meditation routine might be difficult. In this chapter, I lay out a 10-step strategy to help you create and keep up a regular meditation practice. It will be easier to incorporate meditation into your daily life if you follow each step, which is meant to expand your practice gradually.

Step 1: Learn and practice preparing yourself and your space for meditation

Before beginning your meditation practice, setting up a supportive environment is essential. Locate a peaceful area where you can sit quietly and comfortably for the entire session. Stretching, deep breathing, or a little relaxation can help you prepare for this.

Step 2: Appropriate timing and thoughtful refueling

Meditation is often advised to be done in the morning. You can begin the day with clarity and peace thanks to it. While it's ideal to meditate before eating, a small snack can help you focus by keeping your stomach from growling throughout your meditation. Avoid drinking tea or coffee as they could make it difficult for you to relax. Instead, choose a warm beverage like water with lemon to rehydrate and revitalize your body.

Step 3: Start with 10-minute sessions, two to three times a week

Start your meditation journey with brief sessions to ease yourself into the discipline. Two to three times per week, try to sit in meditation for 10 minutes. The key is consistency; by beginning small, you create a base from which you can grow.

Step 4: Create a sacred space and set your intention

Creating a sacred space in your environment can help you develop a supportive mindset for meditation.

Set an intention for your meditation practice before each session. Take a few deep breaths, relax, and close your eyes. Permit yourself to experience inner quiet and flow.

Step 5: Incorporate walking meditation

Consider incorporating walking meditation into your regimen once you've practiced seated meditation for a few weeks. Select a peaceful natural area free from noise and other distractions, and exercise deliberately while embracing the present moment. You develop a deeper awareness of the surroundings and yourself through this activity.

Step 6: Extend sessions to fifteen to thirty minutes five times a week

Increase the length of your meditation sessions progressively as you advance and gain comfort. Five times a week for 15 to 30 minutes is ideal. This extension enables greater reflection and improved advantages.

Step 7: Meditate every day by week eight

Aim to meditate every day by the eighth week. Continue your practice even if scheduling a longer session is difficult. Instead, think about doing shorter, ten-minute meditations to offer your mind and body a chance to relax and reflect.

Step 8: Adapt to your schedule for regularity

If daily meditation feels overwhelming, add it to your schedule. Do it every other day or as often as your commitments permit. Finding a rhythm that works for you will help meditation become a familiar and enduring part of your routine. Consistency is more important than perfection.

Step 9: Treat meditation as a date with yourself

Keep in mind that practicing meditation is a meeting with oneself. Similar to any other significant involvement, treat it as a meaningful commitment. Self-care, inner nurturing, and personal growth are priorities during this time.

Step 10: Daily mindfulness moments

Include attentive moments throughout your day in addition to your regular meditation practice. Every day, set out for three to five minutes for silent thought, free from outside distractions like television, electronics, and other people's voices. Allow yourself to be present as you embrace the silence and reconnect with the present moment.

Consistent meditation practice needs perseverance, commitment, and self-compassion. This 10-step process will help you gradually establish a habit that will provide your life calmness, focus, and balance.

Remember that each level builds on the one before it, allowing you to advance at a rate that fits your unique needs and way of life. Start with brief sessions, progressively lengthen them, and strive for everyday practice. Accept establishing intentions, creating a sacred space, and applying mindfulness to your everyday life.

Through meditation, you can create a closer relationship with yourself, more self-awareness, and a stronger sense of inner peace, in addition to the immediate benefits of relaxation and stress reduction. You will experience the transformative power of meditation in your life if you make a constant effort throughout the journey.

Be kind to yourself as you begin this journey. Your practice may feel difficult on some days, but that's okay. Accept those times with compassion and without judgment. Remember that the goal of meditation is not perfection but to embrace the journey of self-discovery and self-care.

So, commit to following your 10-step plan to establish a regular meditation practice, and watch as it seamlessly integrates into your daily schedule. Accept the silence within, let go of outside distractions, and allow yourself to gain greatly from meditation.

Take advantage of this chance to set out on a journey of self-transformation to discover inner harmony and peace despite the craziness of daily life. You can develop a regular meditation practice; start doing so now to see the wonderful benefits it may have on your health.

CONCLUSION

"By arising in faith and watchfulness, by self-reflection and self-harmony, the wise man makes an island for his soul which many waters cannot overflow."– Buddha

After reading this book, you now understand these powerful techniques and how they can change your life. The ideas of mindfulness and meditation have been thoroughly examined throughout this book, along with the advantages and applications of each. Here are the most important lessons to remember as you reflect on your journey.

Mindfulness and meditation open the door to a more present and satisfying life. By practicing mindfulness, you can develop your ability to be fully present in each experience as it arises. Meditation lets you learn how to quiet your mind, improve your focus, and build a profound sense of serenity. When taken together, they enable you to approach life with more awareness and openness.

The capacity of meditation to treat conditions like stress, anxiety, and depression is one of its most amazing features. As you practice, you learn that your thoughts and feelings are transient and that you can recognize and let go of unfavorable habits. You acquire the ability to control these situations through regular meditation, allowing you to live a more peaceful and balanced life.

You are also encouraged by mindfulness to embrace your inner silence. You can access a source of quiet by letting the outside distractions drift away. Within this silence is the tremendous healing and self-discovery that can take place. You connect with your inner knowledge and find consolation in the depths of your being when you immerse yourself in solitude.

Meditation needs dedication and regular practice. By creating a habit, you provide yourself with a special place to care for your physical and mental health. You will eventually come to understand this practice's transformational potential. You will gain new clarity and insight through meditation by viewing things from a different angle. Regular practice allows you to gain a profound awareness of meditation's advantages for your physical and mental health.

Be kind to yourself as you go on this journey of self-discovery and personal development. It is more important to embrace the process than to achieve perfection. With each step, you advance in clarity, wisdom, happiness, and peace.

Remember when you close this book that mindfulness and meditation practices can significantly improve your mental health and general well-being. You can acquire clarity, wisdom, happiness, and tranquility through commitment and perseverance. So, inhale deeply, widen your heart, and start this amazing journey of inner growth and self-discovery. May meditation and mindfulness lead you to a life filled with joy and contentment, and may your journey be one of peace.

REFERENCES

Ademarsh, & Ramananda, S. (2021). A Step-By-Step Guide to Practicing Mantra Meditation. *Yoga Journal.*

Anahana. (2022, August 25). Do Nothing Meditation. *Meditating With Minimal Effort.* https://www.anahana.com/en/wellbeing-blog/do-nothing-meditation?hs_amp=true

Astin, J. A. (1997). Stress Reduction through Mindfulness Meditation. *Psychotherapy and Psychosomatics, 66*(2), 97–106. https://doi.org/10.1159/000289116

Bastos, F., & Bastos, F. (2022, July 28). How Long Does It Take For Meditation To Work - MindOwl. *MindOwl.* https://mindowl.org/how-long-does-it-take-for-meditation-to-work/

Body Scan Meditation - Headspace. (n.d.). Headspace. https://www.headspace.com/meditation/body-scan#

Clarke, G. (2022, November 28). Intention Meditation - How To Use Intentions In Your Meditation Practice - The Yoga Nomads. *The Yoga Nomads.*

Eisler, M. (2016, May 12). *How to Find Time to Meditate - Mindful Minutes.* Mindful Minutes.

Four Tips for Sticking to a Meditation Practice. (n.d.). Greater Good.

Goyal, M., Singh, S., Sibinga, E. M., Gould, N. F., Rowland-Seymour, A., Sharma, R., Berger, Z., Sleicher, D., Maron, D. J., Shihab, H. M., Ranasinghe, P. D., Linn, S., Saha, S., Bass, E. B., & Haythornthwaite, J. A. (2014b). Meditation Programs for Psychological Stress and Well-being. *JAMA Internal Medicine*, *174*(3), 357.

Greene, P. (2021, March 10). *How long should you meditate? -- By Paul Greene, Ph.D.*Manhattan Center for Cognitive Behavioral Therapy.

Gutierrez, J. (2018, May 29). How to Meditate Daily and Form a Lasting Habit - Better Humans. *Medium*.

Hoge, E. A., Bui, E., Marques, L., Metcalf, C. A., Morris, L., Robinaugh, D. J., Worthington, J. J., Pollack, M. H., & Simon, N. M. (2013). Randomized Controlled Trial of Mindfulness Meditation for Generalized Anxiety Disorder. *The Journal of Clinical Psychiatry*, *74*(08), 786–792. https://doi.org/10.4088/jcp.12m08083

How Meditation Affects Your Brain and Boosts Well-Being. (2021, January 27). Right as Rain by UW Medicine. https://rightasrain.uwmedicine.org/mind/well-being/science-behind-meditation

Insight Timer. (2021). Beyond Asana: The Benefits of Yoga Before Meditation. *Insight Timer Blog*.

Majsiak, B. (2022, June 23). *A Beginner's Guide to Breath Work Practices*. EverydayHealth.com.

MasterClass. (2021a, March 3). *How to Do a Body Scan Meditation: 5 Body Scan Tips - 2023 - MasterClass.*

MasterClass. (2021b, March 3). *Walking Meditation Guide: How to Meditate While Walking - 2023 - MasterClass.*

Meditation and Mindfulness: What You Need To Know. (n.d.). NCCIH. https://www.nccih.nih.gov/health/meditation-and-mindfulness-what-you-need-to-know

Meditation Difficulties - Counseling Center - Loyola University Maryland. (n.d.).

Mukhwana, J., & Grebeniuk, I. (2022). 6 Common Meditation Challenges And How To Overcome Them. *BetterMe Blog.*

Nunez, K. (2020, August 10). *The Benefits of Progressive Muscle Relaxation and How to Do It.* Healthline. https://www.healthline.com/health/progressive-muscle-relaxation#beginner-tips

Omega Institute. (2014). Nature Meditation 101. *eomega.org.* https://www.eomega.org/article/nature-meditation-101

Pmp, H. J. B. C. (2021, November 5). *Which Type of Meditation Is Right for Me?*Healthline.

AUTHOR'S NOTE

I've put all my own knowledge and experience of meditation and mindfulness into this book, as well as carrying out extensive research.

I would love it if this book helps you to see that your overall well-being is largely in your own hands, and by using these wonderfully simple tools, you can resolve conditions such as stress or anxiety; meditation practice enables you to take control of how you manage your day-to-day challenges; feel more in control and navigate your way toward inner peace and calm. I truly hope this book will give you the stimulus to do just that.

Your feedback is important to me because not only will I know what you think of the book, but it also helps me improve. I read every review and take every constructive criticism seriously in order to improve my writing and the quality of my books.

Reviews will help others find this book.

Please use the QR code below.

Amazon.com	Amazon.co.uk	Amazon.au

Thank you.

ALSO BY THIS AUTHOR

Improve Your Life Skills Series:

Publishing July 2023

**The Essential Beginner's
Guide to Buddhism**

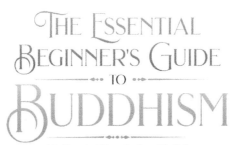

A Guide to the Philosophy; Reveal the Path
to Transforming Your Life; Get Rid of Stress and Anxiety; Achieve
Understanding, Compassion, Wisdom, Calm and Peace

ROHINI HEENDENIYA

Coming Soon in this series:

*Emotional Intelligence
and How to Develop It*

Healing Your Inner Child

Dealing with Toxic Relationships

The Essential Guide to Fasting

Using EFT to Heal Yourself

Spiritual Practice Series:

Publishing July 2023

Tarot Reference Guide,
Workbook and Journal

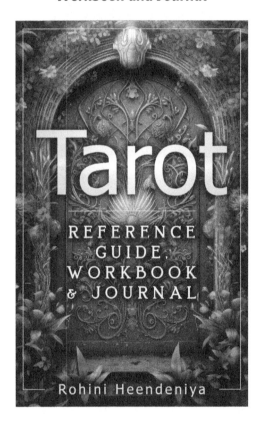

Made in the USA
Las Vegas, NV
26 November 2023

81522201R00105